The Brain Train

Quality Higher Education and Caribbean Development

Hilary McD. Beckles
Anthony Perry
Peter Whiteley

Foreword by Rex Nettleford

A TWENTY-FIRST CENTURY MANIFESTO
The University of the West Indies and Beyond

Board for Undergraduate Studies,
The University of the West Indies, Mona
Kingston 7   Jamaica

© 2002 by Hilary McD. Beckles, Anthony Perry
and Peter Whiteley

Published 2002.

All rights reserved.
No part of this publication may be
reproduced, stored in a retrieval system, or transmitted in
any form, or by any means electronic, photocopying,
recording or otherwise without the
prior permission of the authors.

ISBN 976-41-0194-1

A catalogue record of this book is
available from the National Library of Jamaica

Setin Adobe Garamond 12/15.5 x 27
Cover and book design by Robert Harris
E-mail: roberth@cwjamaica.com
Cover photograph by Ruth Wilson

Printed in Jamaica by Pear Tree Press

Contents

Foreword *v*

Introduction *vii*

Chapter 1   Knowing and Assessing Quality   *1*

Chapter 2   Quality and Higher Education   *8*

Chapter 3   Centring Quality: Enhancing Excellence at UWI   *17*

Chapter 4   New Challenges: E-Learning and Student Centredness   *31*

Chapter 5   Open Access and Quality Issues   *53*

Chapter 6   The Quality Assurance System of UWI   *67*

Chapter 7   Globalization: Internal Quality and External Competition   *78*

Chapter 8   Collaboration or Competition?   *96*

Summary   *104*

Appendix 1   Selected Tertiary Education Quality Assurance Systems   *107*

Appendix 2   Information, Documentation and Data Supplied to a Review Team   *119*

References and Further Reading   *121*

Foreword

For some years now there has been an on-going global debate as to the place of higher education in development. For a developing region like the Caribbean the issue is more precisely the role of quality higher education in its growth and development. Higher education has expanded, both in terms of the numbers engaged in its programmes and in terms of the types of programmes offered. In this context development for the Caribbean region must be seen as encompassing not only economic advancement for the region but also the qualitative changes that lead to a more civil society, with a growing awareness amongst the citizens of the region of their identity as Caribbean people and of their place in the world. The multi-cultural and multi-racial nature of our region continues to provide special challenges and the inculcation of a greater knowledge and appreciation of the cultures of the Caribbean must be a central focus of our education systems. The University of the West Indies (UWI) must ensure that its graduates are not only well trained in their particular disciplines but also sensitive to these various issues, and imbued with a strong sense of social responsibility, in order that they might contribute to the debate.

Knowledge is arguably replacing physical capital as the source of future wealth and higher education now constitutes a primary force driving the sustainability of development. An undergraduate degree impacts positively on the life experiences of its holder. It raises wages and productivity as well as enhancing the quality of civil society and graduates earn more than non-graduates, particularly in the medium to long term. The macro-economic impact of raising the number of those participating in tertiary education is also strong. Just as individuals with better education tend to succeed more in the labour market, so economies with higher tertiary enrolment rates appear to be more dynamic, competitive in global markets, and more successful in terms of higher income per capita. There is also the growing awareness within Caribbean societies that higher education can be seen as a civil right with an attendant demand for inclusion in the benefits of development. The potential for development in the CARICOM community is, however, at risk of being substantially reduced by 'info-poverty', amongst other factors. It is now recognised that the Caribbean lags far behind East Asia, Europe and North America in the number of students in higher education and, in response, CARICOM has targeted a cohort enrolment target of 15% by 2005.

There is also a strong regional tradition that tertiary education should transcend cognitive and intellectual development and should use the teaching and learning environment and experience to develop the character, autonomy and maturity of the whole person. Universities and colleges should not be just teaching and training academies but places for critical thinking, social reflection and scientific development. The preparation of students for citizenship and employability must focus on social capital development in the areas of health, social relations and citizenship. The region must also actively embrace the philosophy of "lifelong learning" as an important organising principle and a prerequisite of a knowledge-based economy.

This book explores in detail many of the issues outlined above and is therefore a timely contribution to the on-going regional debate as to appropriate future directions for education and development. It represents a valuable contribution to the discourse and presents both criticism and self-criticism. Organisations need to periodically review, retool and revise their modus operandi to remain useful and vibrant and the University of the West Indies continues to be engaged in this process of self-evaluation and change.

I commend the Office of Undergraduate Studies on this welcome initiative.

R.M. Nettleford
Vice Chancellor

Introduction

The Brain Train

The Brain Train is the only dependable vehicle on which Caribbean people can journey deeply into the development culture of postmodernity. Nothing short of an education revolution, located primarily in the higher level of the sector, will be adequate. Mass access to quality higher education – the "Brain Train" – is the Caribbean's last chance to secure sustainable development.

The brain drain must be reversed to a place where the Brain Train can be boarded. This is the best way for Caribbean people to effectively gather and focus their abundant intellectual and creative resources in their continuing flight from poverty, dependency, and to counter the growing post-independence sense of disillusionment.

The scientific mobilization of the Caribbean sense of self and sovereignty is a precondition for boarding the Brain Train. The creation of a development-oriented mentality within a learning society is the product of the process. The call here is for popular participation in development thinking and action by opening access to all for relevant higher education. Finding the solutions to challenges faced by Caribbean nation states in this phase of globalization is no simple matter, but the best place to begin the search is on this terrain. The Brain Train is about education and creativity, not certification and validation. It is about the manufacture of creative minds than find fertile expression in the field of the productivist consciousness.

[The Brain drain must be reversed to a place where the Brain Train can be boarded. This is the best way for Caribbean people to effectively gather and focus their abundant intellectual and creative resources in their continuing flight from poverty, dependency, and to counter the growing post-independence sense of disillusionment]

[The Brain Train is about education and creativity, not certification and validation. It is about the manufacture of creative minds than find fertile expression in the field of the productivist consciousness]

Rising Demand

Caribbean societies, as elsewhere, are experiencing an upsurge in the demand for access to quality higher education; hence the need for a scientific quality assurance approach within the sector. Proficiency in knowledge-related skills and the ability to handle information are critical characteristics of this quality education revolution that typifies postmodernity.

Only higher education institutions, universities and others, can produce citizens with generic post-industrial skills of varied kinds in large numbers. But they cannot do so efficiently unless a quality assurance culture is developed as an endemic aspect of the academic environment.

As higher education enrolment increases, the demand for quality will grow. A quality and quality assurance culture, then, is vital to an effectively managed growth process. The establishment of the Quality Assurance Unit at the University of the West Indies (UWI) in 2002 was based on the validity of these arguments. This publication is the result of the many debates and research projects undertaken by the group that constitutes the Quality Assurance team at UWI.

The Caribbean Challenge

The Caribbean is challenged to participate actively in the quality assurance revolution. The number of students in higher education in the world increased from 51 million in 1980 to about 82 million in 1998. It currently stands at about 115 million. In the Caribbean/Latin America area the number of students in higher education per 100,000 inhabitants increased from 1,375 in 1980 to 1,714 in 1995. It now stands at about 2,150. In East Asia the percentage increase was 116.8 per cent and in Europe 74.4 per cent.

When the Caribbean data are disaggregated from Latin America, however, a disturbingly low enrolment ratio is revealed. With respect to the English-speaking subregion the enrolment ratio (number enroled as a percentage of the 20 to 24 age cohort) is less than 10 per cent, compared with an average Latin America ratio of some 30 per cent.

The importance of these data is that they show there is a clear correlation between the level of participation in higher education and economic development, which on average is 51 per cent in the Organization for Economic Cooperation and Development Countries compared with 6 per cent in low-income countries.

The Importance of Relevance

Debates on higher education expansion have shown clearly, furthermore, that the concept of the university as an apolitical international institution is largely a myth. Universities are essentially "national" institutions designed and created to fulfil specific "national" purposes. While UWI is designated a regional university in the geopolitical sense, it is very much a university of the Caribbean nation in the ideological sense.

Easy access to university education is now included in a wider package of civic rights and democratic entitlements in postmodernity. Most universities are seen as relevant – that is, in possession of quality programmes – only when they meet a broad range of national needs.

While enhancing international academic standards, UWI is seeking to become more of a relevant institution. It is not simply that it should be more aggressive in paying attention to regional students, in a geographical sense, but rather that it should know more keenly what the regional needs are and be committed to meeting them. There continues to be considerable agreement on one issue: that UWI is the most important pedagogical force for the achievement of a new strategy of economic and social transformation and development in the subregion.

A Broad Consensus

There is broad consensus also on the view that the future of the English-speaking subregion will depend to a large extent on their capacity to maximize, with the help of UWI, the generation of relevant, new knowledge. The expectations to which UWI, the network of technical and professional institutes, and other tertiary level institutions are subject today require the redefinition of intellectual relationships, systems of academic cooperation, management articulation and the possible creation of institutional mergers. Only a consensual strategy, in which each institution commits resources and efforts, will enable a quality product to emerge.

Quality assurance approaches are more likely to be successful if they are generated from within the institutions themselves than if they were imposed, or simplistically based on alien institutional models. The challenge lies in the self-assessment of institutions in order that they satisfy the demands and deficiencies of Caribbean society, preserving the wealth of traditions, the cultural values, and the great diversity and creativeness of its people.

The consideration of a quality assurance culture within the operation of UWI involves not only organizational and institutional issues but also an assessment of the very processes and purposes of higher education. In examining the future of higher education in the region, a fundamental item must be its role in the education system as a whole.

Acute Problems

The sense of urgency that informs this examination relates to the evidence that shows that the principal obstacle, and drag on Caribbean development, is a shortage of adequately trained, qualified and innovative citizens. This sets the subregion apart from countries whose economic models it seeks to emulate, even if as political rhetoric. In all of this, the finance discourse is important, particularly as a political issue. Who will pay, how, when and how much?

As the demand for quality higher education continues to grow rapidly, leaders in the sector and in government will encounter new problems in gaining greater public support for expansion. For this reason, UWI and other institutions must survive and be willing to fight to survive. In the end, however, success will come to those institutions that do the best job of linking academic activities that operate within them to the survival strategies of citizens.

For UWI, the problems will be acute. The first cause is the tendency of unit costs in higher education to rise faster than unit costs in the overall economy, a tendency accelerated by the rapidly increasing costs of technology. The second cause is the increasing scarcity of public revenue – a function, in turn, of competition from other public needs.

The Way Ahead

The way ahead, the vision, then, should be clearly set out. Part of the effective approach of the 1990s has been an institutional diversification strategy whereby the social demand for quality higher education is managed through the development of various lower cost alternative institutions differentiated in terms of missions, function and modes of delivery. This is well reflected in the increasing trend towards distance learning programmes along with community colleges, polytechnics, and adult and continuing education schools.

One question to be answered is whether the more successful of these institutions should graduate to the status of a university college. On this issue public discourse has revealed that there are three types of ambitions and/or anxieties:

- a public desire for multiple university (degree-granting) bodies within the community;

- the belief in some communities that development requires the existence of a constitutionally established, singularly owned, local/national university; and
- the belief in some societies that these objectives may be met with or without UWI.

But there are also three types of constraints/problems:

- the inability of many of our societies to meet effectively financial obligations to UWI as the regional academy;
- recognition that a "quality university" institution is not built overnight, and it requires massive and long-term social and economic commitment; and
- inadequate human resource capability with respect to delivering an effective institution.

Policy Perspective

The data emanating from its internal quality assurance system, and external scrutiny, suggest that UWI must, in the medium term, reinvent itself once again, in order to continue to be keenly pertinent and effective. What is called for goes beyond limited strategic adjustments but signals the possibility of a major redesign in order to deliver on its strategic objectives.

Significant increases in enrolment are called for as a means to lower per capita costs and improve on efficiency gains. Yet, with no significant funds in hand, or in sight, for infrastructure expansion, an obvious result will be overcrowding in faculties and consequent threats to quality. Furthermore, within this circumstance, students have been asked to pay significantly higher fees. Not surprisingly, intra-faculty relations have become more tense and administrative environments more stressful. An equally disturbing trend is that the rate of enrolment within the faculties targeted for growth – science and technology – has fallen off somewhat.

While enrolment in distance education programmes and at tertiary level institutions are projected as a critical mechanism for growth in student registration, the regional character of UWI, measured in terms of campus interactions among nationals of the region, has also fallen deeper into crisis. A danger is that the regional identity of the university may be sacrificed on the alter of expansion through distance teaching and the formation of a multi-institutional network. Higher educational delivery at the bachelor's level has taken on an overt local hue. The upgrading of any tertiary level institution to university college status may therefore be a deepening rather than a reversal of this trend.

Reinventing UWI

The tension between the idealized concept of UWI as a regional institution and the reality of student enrolment patterns is one that can only be eased, given the harsh circumstances of educational economics – for both students and stakeholders – at the level of graduate studies. The debate here is likely to revolve around the notion that the traditional campuses could focus more on graduate training in terms of resource development. But the fact is that the enormous infrastructural investments on campuses are best suited to mass undergraduate teaching, and this is factored into the strategic plans of campuses in terms of human resource development trajectories.

These tensions must be understood and diffused by creative innovations, especially in the area of institutional redesign. The issue of capacity building remains critical, and maybe one or two of the tertiary level institution vehicles on which we have travelled in the past decade or so require some upgrading to university college status in order to be self-sustainable. It may also be true that resources not readily available to UWI (as we know it now) may be placed at the disposal of a local institution designated a university college.

Benchmarking

The critical issues of quality assurance and benchmarking standards reside at the fore of the discussion. Quality is about relevance and fitness for purpose. The university is just beginning to approach quality assurance within the wider context of distance education and tertiary level institution delivery. For this reason it will be strategic at this time to develop an aggressive macro-perspective that embraces all programmes within the university network.

This publication, then, is offered as a contribution to the discourse. It is presented to you with the hope that it serves as a site of reflection, a signpost, better yet, along a journey that will be testing of stamina and turbulent in its duration.

1 Knowing and Assessing Quality

Introduction

In the Caribbean and beyond, universities have long considered that they represent high quality and standards in education. In so thinking they have evolved in terms of their mandates and reasons for being. Different traditions and procedures have developed to maintain and demonstrate the standards and quality of provision in different countries.

One such procedure has been the articulation of internal self-assessment with external scrutiny. The external accreditation procedures used universally in the higher education sector in North America, and in the professional faculties of UWI, contrast with the methods used in the British university sector.

Historically, the British university procedure centred on intra-university processes (for curriculum changes, for instance), inter-university contacts (such as using external examiners to evaluate examination content and marking standards) and, on a broader level, professional contacts (such as academic conferences).

In recent years, however, more formal, external methods have been instituted in Britain. Universities are now big businesses and they have not escaped the pressures on all businesses to provide quality products in an efficient manner, including establishing good management practices and using resources with flexibility. In addition, there is now an array of financial difficulties in many higher education systems resulting from a relative decrease in public sector financial support.

[Universities are now big businesses and have not escaped the pressures on all businesses to provide quality products in an efficient manner]

Quality Movement

These and other pressures have led to a worldwide "quality" movement in education, including the development and adoption of formal quality assurance and audit systems. During the last decade there have been

[These and other pressures have led to a worldwide "quality" movement in education]

rapid developments and greater expectations have arisen for the presentation of clear and independent evidence of the quality of the education being provided by higher education institutions.

Further, as the demand for higher education has grown, and consequently the number of students entering colleges and universities has risen, concern has been expressed about both the quality of the provision for the students and the output standards of the institutions, leading to a growing need for institutions to accommodate a greater level of accountability. Although the debate as to the most appropriate perspective on the nature of educational quality is by no means over, it is now generally accepted that there is need for greater transparency and increased public discussion of the work of higher education institutions.

Industrial versus Educational Quality

Customer-centred definitions of quality are widely accepted throughout industry. Customer perception and opinion are often seen as the key elements in defining the quality of a product or service. In an industrial setting, quality may be seen as "meeting the customers' needs", with the organizational effort directed towards raising the quality of the product by modifications to suit the customers' perceived or stated needs.

[It must be noted that in higher education it can be difficult to precisely identify who is the customer]

While this model points to the importance of educational institutions seeking out and accepting feedback from its stakeholders, it must be noted that in higher education it can be difficult to precisely identify who is the customer. Is the student the "real" customer or is it necessary to take account of the wishes of employers, governments or even parents?

Product or Service?

[The product provided by an educational institution is an intangible service]

The product provided by an educational institution is an intangible service, and the production and consumption of the service often occur simultaneously. The teaching and learning processes are difficult to control in the way industrial inputs and processes can be controlled. Indeed, many educational inputs cannot be controlled to any substantial degree: the consumer (the student) is an important part of the input and often the direct involvement of the consumer and producer (the lecturer/tutor) is needed for "production" to take place.

Industrial concepts of quality are often also linked with conformity with given specifications. The specification of a service comprises many standards; quality is measured in terms of the degree to which the service matches the specifications. Such specification, however, assumes that the service can be validly defined in terms of parameters that are measurable and quantifiable.

[Quality is measured in terms of the degree to which the service matches the specifications]

In education there are also problems of interpretation, even when a chosen parameter may have validity in itself. For example, when the numbers of degrees in each class are considered, the awarding of greater numbers of first-class degrees in an institution may indicate either the raising or lowering of standards.

Performance Indicators

Governments often explicitly or implicitly use a quality model that involves "value for money" in which "greater efficiency" is demanded. In higher education institutions this may lead to the use of quantitative performance indicators to assess the institutions. These indicators may include the staff/student ratios; the qualifications of the entrants and their examination results; the proportion of entrants completing the programmes and the average time taken; the number of graduates unemployed six months after graduating; ratings of teaching, and so on.

[Care must be taken to avoid drawing unwarranted inferences and incorrectly assuming causal factors]

Such indicators must be considered within the context of the resources available and related to the objectives of the programmes. Appropriate interpretation is important and care must be taken to avoid drawing unwarranted inferences and incorrectly assuming causal factors. Quantitative performance indicators are better used as data within a broader quality assessment process.

The Assessing Culture

Everyone gets assessed these days. Students, of course, come in for the deepest exposure to assessment. From admissions through to graduation, there is systematic assessment of students. The assumption is that if colleges and universities perfect the business of assessing their students, then some sort of excellence is achieved. More recently, though, students have been on the other side of assessment.

[More recently, though, students have been on the other side of assessment]

Students now assess lecturers. End-of-course evaluation of teaching is widely used. Academics, additionally, subject their colleagues to some of the most rigorous and detailed assessments when a colleague comes up for tenure or promotion. Administrators also get in on the action. In many institutions, administrators have the final say on who gets hired and who is denied tenure. Administrators also assess each other. Finally, every element of the institution gets assessed. But to what end? Is assessment indicative of excellence and the quality of higher education? And who benefits from assessment results?

[Is assessment indicative of excellence and the quality of higher education?]

What Is Assessed

Assessment efficiency can be impeded when not everyone is sure about what is being accomplished. Academics are clear, it is believed, that they know why they assess their students. It is not so clear, though, that students always understand why, how or even when they are being assessed. Some would go further to suggest that assessment results do not give a true or reliable picture of academic promise or achievement.

Some writers argue that much of what is done in assessment is practised out of habit, for convenience, and to carry out administrative duties. Should not the real reason be about how well academics and administrators provide students with the opportunities to excel and how the institution achieves quality in its teaching and learning provision?

[It is not so clear, though, that students always understand why, how or even when they are being assessed]

Limits of Assessing

The premise on which quality assessment practices have been built is that the values of the institution are reflected in the information gathered by academics and administrators on the quality of the academic enterprise. That quality, demonstrated though teaching, research and public service, is used to measure the degree to which excellence has been achieved and the extent to which the goals of the academy have been realized. Yet many students do not fully embrace the same set of values that are espoused by their teachers and administrators.

Quality, however, is not always evident through the research, scholarly activities and public service because, important as these elements may be to the academy, they are not always as significant to students. Public opinion and perception of excellence and quality are sometimes at variance with opinion and perception within the academy.

[Many students do not fully embrace the same set of values that are espoused by their teachers and administrators]

Divided Audience

Within the academy, too, there is some doubt about the way students' achievements are assessed. Teachers receive recognition for their research and public service, but it does not always follow that students believe that they are beneficiaries of the quality and excellence applauded.

Excellence is expected in the classroom and quality is measured by the extent to which students are motivated and are helped to know how well they are doing. Assessment should not be seen as separate from the everyday business of teaching and learning or as something only to be undertaken when the programme has been completed.

In its broadest sense, assessment seeks to take an inventory of the entire process as academics and administrators seek to find ways to assure and enhance the quality of educational provision. Assessment focuses more on outcomes rather than on input. If we wish to know how the academy is performing, we can find evidence in the work of students.

Quality Is Core

Quality assurance is but one of the elements of the assessment of excellence within the academy. In the United States it is called "accreditation". Whatever the term, assessment can conjure up negative images for students and burdensome realities for academics and administrators. That UWI has chosen a "fitness for purpose" definition of quality means that there is a requirement to move beyond describing aims and objectives of cognate disciplines and address some interrelated questions that surface around the assessment of student achievement.

Targeting Excellence

The future of quality higher education in the Caribbean will depend upon the extent to which stakeholders are able to document the relevance and effectiveness of the programmes and services that are provided. To a large extent, quality assurance reviews utilize systems of programme assessment that are credible and meaningful. Included in the group of constituents are students who are central in assuring quality.

[Excellence is expected in the classroom and quality is measured by the extent to which students are motivated and are helped to know how well they are doing]

[Assessment focuses more on outcomes rather than on input. If we wish to know how the academy is performing, we can find evidence in the work of students]

[By conducting quality assurance reviews, universities are committing themselves to the promotion of excellence that must be demonstrated in teaching, research and community service]

Quality assurance, therefore, must assess the extent to which access to higher education is aligned with external client and societal needs.

By conducting quality assurance reviews, universities are committing themselves to the promotion of excellence that must be demonstrated in teaching, research and community service. Traditional views of excellence require the assumption that finance, a highly qualified staff and high-quality students are the necessary inputs.

Some educators, though, have become critical of traditional conceptions of excellence. Gaining ground is the "talent development" view that more attention should be given to the quality of the experience than to the quality of entering students. The belief that excellence is a function of how well students learn should make us more inclined to assess changes in students' performance over time.

Impact of Rising Enrolment

It is widely believed that massification of higher education has led to the deterioration of both quality and standards. Research suggests that abundant resources might well attract high-quality staff and students but might not necessarily achieve the kinds of outcomes that indicate excellence.

Administrators are likely to opine that highly selective admissions criteria are necessary to assure academic excellence. Expanding intake does not in itself, however, affect an institution's reputation or mean that fewer qualified candidates are accepted. Why is so much emphasis placed on the assessment of admissions? Does recruiting mostly high achievers from the secondary level make a better university?

This assessment approach is often taken one step further in universities: "If so many bright students want to come here, we must be very good." By attracting the "best", then, we should turn out the best. What responsibility do we then have in ensuring excellence in teaching and research? For instance, consider resources. The resource notion of quality means we must seek to provide the requisite teaching/learning experiences that will enhance talent development among the students. Assessment of resources, therefore, must be one of the means by which it is possible to operationalize notions of excellence. The talent development of students can only be nurtured if academics and administrators operate at high standards, despite resource restraint.

Quality and Reviews

Reviews of quality and standards and the assessment of excellence are critical to the reputation of the academy. Assessment practices should further the basic aims and objectives of higher education. Assessment, quality reviews and evaluation must outline and explain the purposes and value of university education. Universities should account to stakeholders the raison d'être of higher education. The reputational view of excellence is based on the idea that institutions of high quality are the ones that enjoy the best academic reputation.

External constituents are questioning the role of the university, often calling for a movement away from traditionally delivered instruction and for greater efficiency and wider access. Employers are increasingly expressing dissatisfaction with the skills and competencies, attitudes and social consciousness that graduates bring into the workplace.

The quality of instruction at UWI has come under greater scrutiny in the past few years. Its relevance as the leading regional teaching and research institution is subject to systematic assessment. Scientific approaches to collecting and using assessment data have helped to answer many questions about the university and have provided greater transparency to those within who are oftentimes as strongly critical as those on the outside.

[Reviews of quality and standards and the assessment of excellence are critical to the reputation of the academy]

Quality and Higher Education

A useful distinction can be made between the quality of the provision of an institution and the standards of the awards from the institution. The provision includes the programmes and courses offered; the resources available; the teaching, learning and assessment methods used; and so on.

The standards of an institution are linked with the stated learning objectives and the learning outcomes. Thus a student may reach a good standard in his or her coursework, projects and examinations in spite of inadequacies in institutional provision. Any evaluation of the programmes of an institution needs to include consideration of both the level of provision and of the learning outcomes.

[A useful distinction can be made between the quality of the provision of an institution and the standards of the awards from the institution]

Terminology

In higher education, "quality assurance" has come to be used as an all-embracing term to include all the policies, processes and actions of higher education institutions, agencies and organizations through which the quality of higher education is maintained and developed. Included in these processes are evaluation and accreditation.

"Evaluation" is a systematic, critical analysis of the quality of an object or system. In higher education it is concerned with the quality of the:

- goals of higher education (for example, institutional mission, aims of a programme);

- inputs into higher education (for example, physical and human resources, students on entry);

- processes used within higher education (for example, teaching and assessment procedures); and

- outcomes of higher education (for example, attitudes, skills, understanding and knowledge possessed by students at graduation; research publications).

Evaluating Education

Evaluation of a higher education institution may focus on one or more of the following:

- Teaching and learning
- Research and scholarship
- Contribution to the community
- The institution as a whole, including its management and strategic planning

[Evaluation can be applied to individuals, programmes, subjects or discipline areas, departments, faculties, and institutions]

Evaluation can be applied to individuals, programmes, subjects or discipline areas, departments, faculties, and institutions. Evaluation normally has an internal dimension (self-evaluation) and an external dimension (by external experts, by peers or by inspectors). *Quality assessment* or *quality measurement* are often used synonymously to evaluation, particularly if there is an external element. Quality assurance systems within an institution, however, do not necessarily involve accreditation.

Accreditation is primarily an outcome of evaluation. Accreditation is the award of a status and signals approval, recognition and sometimes a licence to operate. Accreditation as a process is generally based on the application of predefined expectations and criteria.

Components of Quality Assurance Systems

[Quality assurance systems in universities often display commonalities]

Quality assurance systems in universities often display commonalities even though the institutions are set in very different cultures and possess very different histories. Some of these components are outlined below.

[Committees outside the department concerned should monitor the revision and updating of courses]

Within universities there are usually thorough procedures for the development and approval of new courses and programmes. It is, however, important to note that the currency, relevance and appropriateness of programmes must be adequately maintained and this may be more difficult to achieve. For instance, there can be resistance from the teaching staff to the discontinuation of particular courses. Committees outside the department concerned should monitor the revision and updating of courses.

✣ Standards

Three central considerations in the maintenance of standards in universities are the examination system itself, the entry levels of students and the exit levels of graduates:

- The integrity of the examination system is central to any university and there must be explicit written examination procedures, regulations and safeguards.

- Entry requirements should be regularly reviewed, along with undertaking analyses of relationships between the entry level and the level of qualification obtained. With pressures to increase enrolment, the students' entry levels must be appropriate for the programmes. If increased access to university programmes is desired, the development of new programmes suitable for students at different entry levels is preferable to reducing the entry standards into the current programmes.

- Establishing and maintaining appropriate standards for the various qualifications is a major issue for universities. External examiners are often used, and comments are obtained from senior academics within other universities on the suitability of the examinations and standards.

[With pressures to increase enrolment, the students' entry levels must be appropriate for the programmes]

[Establishing and maintaining appropriate standards for the various qualifications is a major issue for universities]

✣ Resources

Universities require both physical and human resources. The physical resources, such as information technology, may be relatively easily upgraded (by simple acquisition) if they are inadequate for the programmes being offered. However, it can be substantially more difficult to ensure that the professional development of staff is adequate and that sufficient resources are committed to this purpose, particularly due to the longer term nature of the gain for the university. Allied to this is the need to conduct appraisals of staff members for formative and developmental purposes; it is not adequate for staff only to be assessed for promotional considerations. Further, adequate technical and administrative personnel support for teaching staff needs to be provided.

[Adequate technical and administrative personnel support for teaching staff needs to be provided]

✣ Feedback

Research by universities into the opinions of its stakeholders is important to order to remain relevant and responsive to their concerns. Universities need to establish procedures and structures to receive and respond to feedback from its current students, graduates, employers of the graduates, the government and other related groups, such as professional associations.

The following are some methods for obtaining feedback:

- Student course evaluation instruments, staff/student liaison committees, formal student representation at all levels of the university
- Meetings with industry and employers of graduates
- Periodic surveys of recent graduates and employers
- Obtaining external professional comment on programme content

Publication of mission statements, strategic plans, and aims and objectives demands a thorough system of public reporting. These reports should then allow the institution to demonstrate to its stakeholders how its short-, medium- and longer-term objectives are being achieved. All aspects of an institution's work should undergo periodic review, including the governance and management of the institution, although this does not appear to be central in many universities. A governing body, however constituted, has a responsibility for the appointment, development and appraisal of the senior management that is then responsible for implementing and initiating policies agreed on by the governing body and for the efficient and effective management of the institution.

✣ Self-Evaluation

Self-evaluation (which may also be described as self-study or self-assessment) is usually the first stage in the process of an institutional, departmental or subject evaluation. When the system has as its next stage an evaluation by an external group, the report of the self-evaluation may provide a framework for the external evaluation. In other cases, the results of the self-evaluation should feed directly into institutional decision making.

As the first step in the overall process, the self-evaluation of the institution or of particular programmes can be seen to have three major purposes:

- to present a succinct and comprehensive statement of the academic staff members' perspective on the programmes being offered;
- to analyse the strengths and weaknesses of the programmes and to propose action plans; and

[Universities need to establish procedures and structures to receive and respond to feedback from its current students, graduates, employers of the graduates, the government and other related groups, such as professional associations]

[All aspects of an institution's work should undergo periodic review, including the governance and management of the institution, although this does not appear to be central in many universities]

[In other cases, the results of the self-evaluation should feed directly into institutional decision making]

- to provide a framework within which a group of external experts may assess the programmes.

Reporting Results

The self-evaluation process results in a report describing the programme and offering critical reflection as to how it is managed and how quality is handled. Self-evaluation reports should be both descriptive and analytical; the reports should evaluate strengths and weaknesses in the context of constraints and opportunities and show the interconnectedness of the various elements of strategic planning and quality management.

A prerequisite for change is the institutionalization of internal mechanisms of quality assessment and the establishment of durable procedures that ensure public transparency for the outcome of this assessment. A useful approach is a two-stage process for drafting the report so that members of academic staff have to respond to an initial draft, and hence have to decide their own points of view towards the issues in the draft self-evaluation;

[Self-evaluation reports should be both descriptive and analytical]

Reporting as Policy

Self-evaluation reports should indicate the aims and objectives of the teaching programmes. Without these it may be difficult to discern the extent to which the structure of the curriculum and departmental policy are consistent with the aims and objectives. The procedures for quality management are described, as the procedures for evaluating the quality of teaching programmes or individual teachers may differ in different subjects.

Surveys should be undertaken to establish the extent to which graduates and employers are content with the programmes, and this information obtained is useful in analysing the quality of the programmes. The reasons for dissatisfaction and satisfaction can be a good starting point for the overall improvement of the work of a department. Higher education institutions often now issue evaluation forms to students at the end of each course in a programme. The remainder of the self-evaluation report should aim to demonstrate how the aims and objectives are being met by the teaching of the discipline. The report will discuss the curriculum, the teaching and learning methods and opportunities, the student

[Self-evaluation reports should indicate the aims and objectives of the teaching programmes]

[Surveys should be undertaken to establish the extent to which graduates and employers are content with the programmes, and this information obtained is useful in analysing the quality of the programmes]

profile, the assessment methods and learning outcomes, resources for teaching and learning, along with procedures for quality assurance and enhancement.

Strengths and Weaknesses of the Self-Evaluation Process

[The self-evaluation report should aim to demonstrate how the aims and objectives are being met by the teaching of the discipline]

The main strengths of self-evaluation are:

- encouraging all members of academic staff to recognize their responsibility for the quality of teaching and learning;
- developing a critical and analytic view of all activities;
- providing an opportunity to analyse what quality assurance means and to obtain a holistic view of the activities;
- providing an opportunity for the staff to analyse activities and formulate judgements in relation to problems of academic, financial and administrative autonomy;
- providing a source of new and potentially useful ideas for the future;
- providing an opportunity to strengthen current positive actions and identify possible areas for further improvement;
- highlighting different opinions about quality and quality assurance of different members of staff; and
- providing an opportunity for students and teachers to interact and improve communication.

Limits of Self-Review

Weaknesses of self-evaluation include:

- the risk that the self-evaluation may be unrealistic;
- inadequate consideration of the opinions of stakeholders (for example, students, graduates, employers)
- insufficient discussion of its findings within the wider community of staff, students and administration;
- inadequate collation and generalization of ideas;

- inadequate extraction of sufficiently self-reflective and analytic material from existing information (from annual reports and the like); and
- the lack of an action plan to tackle problems identified through the self-evaluation.

Academic staff may find the self-evaluation process potentially valuable, but for this value to be realized on a continuing basis (particularly in the absence of external evaluation as an incentive) it needs to become an integral part of each institution's accepted framework of quality assurance and management. Further, without the capacity to effect change, self-evaluation may satisfy an external team but have little other value. If the process is to have a positive effect then a recognized link must be established between self-evaluation and the institution's decision-making processes.

[Without the capacity to effect change, self-evaluation may satisfy an external team but have little other value]

Effective Procedures

It is also important that institutions develop procedures that are as cost-effective as possible. If the process is to be economical, it should be able to depend upon the existence of reliable and up-to-date information being recorded in the normal course of institutional management and on this information being made readily available. Such data needs to be recorded so that it can easily be analysed for trends, and institutions need to learn the potential that performance indicators have in identifying matters requiring evaluative judgement. It is good practice for the outcome of an internal evaluation to include targets established on a specified time scale and for success in meeting these targets to be monitored in subsequent evaluations.

[It is good practice for the outcome of an internal evaluation to include targets]

✥ *External Evaluation of Programmes*

After the completion of the self-evaluation report, a group of external experts may undertake a site visit. The aims of external evaluations are to form an opinion on the quality management and strategic management capacities of the institution (or section) evaluated, and to make recommendations to improve these capacities. Other aspects of the assignment of an external team may be:

- to form an opinion about the quality of the programme (for example, the educational process, the curricula, the students) on the basis of the self-evaluation report and by means of discussions held during the visit;

- to form an opinion on the relationship between the programme and the mission of the institution and consider the links between teaching and research; and

- to make recommendations to improve the quality of teaching.

Recognizing Achievements

The requirements of the assignment point to a tension under which evaluators may have to work: on the one hand the audit-type remit to judge provision and standards for external publication and, on the other hand, the desire from the institution evaluated to obtain recognition for achievements in teaching and research and to receive advice as to enhancement. Lack of institutional support for the self-evaluation process and suspicious academic staff can make the visit less effective than is desirable. Meetings should take place with the self-evaluation group, heads of department, students, graduates, employers and senior academic and administrative staff members. Visits should also be made to the libraries, teaching accommodation and relevant laboratory and information technology facilities.

[Lack of institutional support for the self-evaluation process and suspicious academic staff can make the visit less effective than is desirable]

⊕ Strengths and Weaknesses of an External Evaluation Process

Potential strengths of an external evaluation are:

- support for the findings of the self-evaluation report strengthens the authority of the staff regarding their analysis of academic activities;

- academic staff can gain a better of understanding of internationally accepted conceptions of quality and of quality assurance procedures;

- external experts are able to identify significant points and make proposals for further development, with critical remarks and suggestions being, at times, more valuable than the positive comments;

- the process can engender positive attitudes among academic staff and strengthen interactions among constituent parts of the university; and

- students may discuss strengths and weaknesses of the academic activities without the presence of their teachers.

Knowing Weaknesses

Potential weaknesses of an external evaluation process are that

- it places additional burdens on staff, although staff involvement is essential;
- the external experts may be unfamiliar with details of the programmes and/or the institution so the evaluation report becomes too general;
- the range of the experts' cultural and professional backgrounds can mean certain problems are only partially explored;
- there may be insufficient involvement of non-academics in the review team; and
- a single evaluation event may be insufficient, with a need for regular events to allow more in-depth discussions of detail.

Survival Strategies

Experience with evaluation in the higher education institutions has historically not been widespread. Simple evaluation methods that in themselves may motivate participants (staff as well as students) to engage in enhancement of teaching and learning are needed: quality improvement will result from involvement, not from inspection. Strategies for survival of national societies and economies are at stake, and higher education should play a role; quality assurance is concerned with playing this role effectively.

The main strengths clearly revolve around the value of bringing an external (and international) perspective to bear on internal findings and on internal processes for quality assurance. A better understanding of international conceptions of quality and recognition of the links between accountability and autonomy in relation to quality assurance are important aspects of these perspectives.

[Experience with evaluation in the higher education institutions has historically not been widespread]

[Quality improvement will result from involvement, not from inspection]

3 Centring Quality
Enhancing Excellence at UWI

[Students and parents have become much more critical of the university experience in light of increased fees]

There has been much discussion among academics, administrators, policy makers and students about the changing nature of academic quality and standards; about deepening and widening access, and effective articulation with the wider sector; and about fiscal accountability. Students and parents have become much more critical of the university experience in light of increased fees and the perceived threats to the quality of the learning environment.

These issues must occupy more keenly the thinking and action of management teams if we are to advance the interests of the community served by UWI. Stakeholders have become far more critical of the role and function of UWI, particularly as they expect it to maintain its reputation as the leading higher education institution in the region. They have been paying greater attention to monetary contributions, and there are UWI graduates who have begun to express dissatisfaction with the quality of some programmes.

[There are UWI graduates who have begun to express dissatisfaction with the quality of some programmes]

Quality at UWI

At the heart of the quality assurance revolution is the extent to which a university can deliver fully on its mission, particularly as it relates to the relevance of its programme. Quality assurance mechanisms and procedures have been adopted in UWI to ensure that what is offered at the Cave Hill, Mona and St Augustine campuses, at its many centres, and in partnership with other tertiary level institutions meets the needs of all stakeholders.

[Universities will rise and fall on the issue of quality]

As an institution of international repute, in a competitive domestic and external environment, UWI participates meaningfully in the global quality assurance discourse found in higher education. UWI seeks much of its recognition for its professional degrees from accrediting bodies in the United Kingdom and is therefore exposed to their rigorous quality assurance culture. Universities will rise and fall on the issue of quality; it is a matter of survival.

Space Constraints

The physical expansion of UWI is challenged to keep pace with the increase in student enrolment. This condition is generating much tension and must therefore be managed creatively. It is critical that attention be paid both quantity and quality.

How can stakeholders be assured that UWI, which produces excellent graduates, continues to provide a high-quality educational experience for the people of the region? How can it balance the need to expand to educate considerably more than 3 per cent of the cohort of post-secondary students with the desire to retain excellence in its programme offerings?

The Challenges

UWI faces a set of serious challenges. The Caribbean lags far behind East Asia, Europe and North America in the number of students enrolled in higher education. Less than 10 per cent of the 20 to 34 age cohort in the English-speaking subregion is enroled in higher education. The hemispheric norm is 35 per cent. In Latin America enrolment is 35 per cent and is rising closer to the North American norm which exceeds 50 per cent.

There are many questions for which answers may not be obvious. How can shareholders tangibly demonstrate their commitment to higher education opportunities to a wider cross-section of the community in the face of fiscal restraint? How can political and corporate leaders in the CARICOM area meet national education targets while at the same time supporting a regional university that still offers too few places?

[The Caribbean lags far behind East Asia, Europe and North America in the number of students enrolled in higher education]

Public Opinion

Some citizens voice strong nationalist views about the type of higher education institutions that would best serve the local needs while clamouring for a regional university that is necessary for social, political and economic transformation. How can these multiple, contradictory positions be aligned to achieve the targets set to bring the region into line with high achievers in the developing world?

Is UWI poised to lead its community to the desired goals of social transformation and poverty alleviation? Will the university in the twenty-first century continue to produce the most able graduates the region can afford? These questions can only be answered and these objectives met with the maintenance of a quality educational system, characterized by excellence in all programmes in whatever mode of delivery, whether on-campus sites, by distance or in collaboration with other tertiary level institutions.

Encouraging Debate

The massification of higher education in the region does not in itself mean a reduction in the quality of our undergraduate programmes. It requires a shift in focus from the input to the output as a part of a strategy to secure a greater commitment to the preservation of the traditions of pedagogical excellence and high cultural values.

YouWe Quality Assurance Forum, the publication of the Board for Undergraduate Studies, was created to articulate views on quality assurance issues and challenges. The years ahead promise to be intellectually challenging. For UWI to be successful in its quality agenda it must facilitate its reinvention in the coming decade.

The necessary response from academic leaders must not be bureaucratically centred or incremental, but intellectually transformative within the context of a new coherent policy for education and training, both of which require effective coordination.

A Sense of Urgency

A noticeable feature of the 1998 fiftieth anniversary celebrations/reflections of the university was the highlighting of the sense of urgency embedded within the UWI Strategic Plan (1997–2002). It was stated explicitly that the institution has not responded with sufficient speed, or at the appropriate level, to the cultural and technological changes now challenging and redefining the youngest generation.

Furthermore, and this much is revealed clearly by recent quality audits carried out by the Office of the Board for Undergraduate Studies, it has not effectively grasped the now compelling philosophy of "lifelong learning" that is the organizing principle of postmodern society and is a prerequisite of the knowledge-based economy.

An insider's perspective suggests, in addition, that UWI is challenged to define and develop innovative forms of teaching and learning. With a principal public mandate to expand student numbers without a corresponding loss of quality, the challenge requires even greater commitment.

The twenty-year-old, unresolved debate on English language proficiency as it relates to access and matriculation, for example, illuminates the divided vision within quality assurance discourse. Only the linguists can provide scientific answers on this issue within the quality assurance framework that must engage the vernacular sensibility.

[The institution has not responded with sufficient speed, or at the appropriate level, to the cultural and technological changes now challenging and redefining the youngest generations]

Role of the Faculties

Faculties at UWI have addressed the need to adapt curricula to respond to new kinds of students and the demands of public services and private industry. They have done so at a time, and within an environment, characterized by the endemic fiscal crisis of supportive nation states and widespread public questioning of the cost and value of university provision.

For these reasons, among others, university leadership is keeping one eye sharply focused on the intellectual and pedagogical issues related to the objectives of social cohesion and social justice while fixing the other on operational policies and programmes designed to enhance economic growth and community development.

The building of new constituencies of public support across regional communities (beyond alumni networks) should follow as a reasonable consequence of the exposure of these new constituencies to relevant, innovative and creative academic programmes. Faculties should seek directly to create lasting links of mutual support with all stakeholders.

[University leadership is keeping one eye sharply focused on the intellectual and pedagogical issues related to the objectives of social cohesion and social justice while fixing the other on operational policies and programmes designed to enhance economic growth and community development]

Commitment to Scholarship

The principal objective should be to nurture a critical understanding of academic and social issues among students, in whatever disciplines they study. The strengthening of commitment to the intellect must be the primary purpose of the faculty. It is within the academic context and institutional circumstance that the refinement and expansion of the system and discourse of quality assurance at UWI was conceived and implemented.

The promotion within communities of a popular desire for "lifelong learning" as a concept, and the basis of a future project, will enable faculties to engage the critical debates relating to "deeper access", "wider access" and "continuing access" to UWI.

Driven by new information and communications technologies, "lifelong learning" curricula speak to the idea of a "learning society" that is self-critical and is inclusive of everyone. It also speaks to the concepts of flexibility, democratization and public empowerment in education, all of which reside at the core of UWI's commitment to quality.

This is no time to be soft on the political philosophy of "Caribbeanness", however. UWI can no longer claim monopoly institutional leadership in the field of knowledge creation in the region: it must happily share the status and responsibility with dozens of other centres, but it must continue to position itself to set the trajectory for identity formation, regional integration and cultural mobilization.

The Tertiary Level Institutions

The re-engineering of the Caribbean tertiary level infrastructure to enable student migration between and across programmes and institutions is a pressing necessity. UWI must continue to seek ways to build new inter-institutional capabilities with the objective of creating an open-ended learning environment for students. Tertiary level institutions will especially require broad-based support as partnerships for degree delivery are established. UWI must facilitate the necessary initiatives for the Caribbean educational network to be developed as a common student reality.

By necessity, any relevant inter-institutional student culture should transcend the anglophone space and focus on the common identity and interest of the entire region. Exploiting fully the many collaborative agreements in existence with universities throughout the region, in order to normalize "free" movement within the multilingual teaching and learning environment, must be a pressing objective. In this regard, a quality education calls for the promotion of foreign-language skills as a student right rather than a privilege.

[The strengthening of commitment to the intellect must be the primary purpose of the faculty]

[This is no time to be soft on the political philosophy of "Caribbeanness"]

[UWI must continue to seek ways to build new inter-institutional capabilities with the objective of creating an open-ended learning environment for students]

The effective use of advanced information and communications technologies is critical. Foreign-language proficiency and computer literacy are as vital to the development of the Caribbean teaching and learning environment as any other set of skills and resources. They are interlinked and require student competence in order to assure stakeholders of the quality of university provisions.

Student Centredness

UWI is in the process, like many universities worldwide, of reinventing itself in order confront this millennium equipped with the methods and values of the postmodern university. A student-centred university environment is one in which students are the principal focus. In such an environment all activities and programmes are ultimately viewed from the standpoint of their impact on students and particularly on student learning. As has been noted, student centredness cannot be equated with student friendliness: it is a larger concept, in that some actions – for example, enforcing a ban on loud music in halls of residence – might be seen as unfriendly, but, ultimately, they are student centred when viewed in terms of developing students' respect for the rights of others.

This does not diminish in any way the importance of student friendliness as a standard for service to and interaction with students. Thus only a student-centred and student-friendly university can effectively serve the people of the region in the years ahead. So far, the process of centring students has been slow and painful, but the trajectory is clear. If one fact must be fully understood and located at the centre, it is this: the core of the academy is the student body.

Some areas have witnessed considerable progress, while others are hampered by a crippling inertia that is rooted in the traditional, vertical teacher-centred culture. This authoritarian, hierarchal culture, so endemic to the process of colonialism, has fashioned an elitist pedagogical value system within the academy. Only freedom from this traditional power relation, and its administrative structures that have served to enforce student subordination, will secure teacher-student relations that are based on academic mutualism.

The global process of student centring is driven by many considerations that have significance for quality assurance. UWI, long the sole light rising in our west, is now surrounded by a growing constellation of institutions that see no reason to defer to the senior partner now cast as principal competitor. The struggle for potential students has become a bitter one in some areas, and individual purchasers of education are not only shopping around but in most cases are setting out the terms of their purchase and the conditions of consumption.

Student Friendliness

Any institution that does not display and assure quality, and offer value and high standards, will be uncompetitive and may not survive. Student friendliness is the hallmark of good quality and is one benchmark by which an institution's competitive edge is measured. If the student is not willing to be associated with the academy as an alumnus, nor to recommend the experience to potential students, then certainly there is a crisis of quality and loss of competitiveness will follow.

UWI has already grasped the full meaning of these issues. In many ways it is now a matured academy that feels within its bones how best to move rapidly in order to secure its future. It has been blessed with effective leadership for most of its fifty years and has the tools with which to chart its future as a leader in student-centred pedagogy.

[Any institution that does not display and assure quality, and offer value and high standards, will be uncompetitive]

Welcoming Students

The student must feel welcomed, wanted and empowered in all areas of the environment: in the faculty and departmental offices, the registry, library, bookstore, and lecture theatres. Wherever students go, the feeling must be communicated to them that UWI is here to serve their development needs. Their right to critically assess programmes and teaching must be institutionalized as a norm in every faculty, as this is one way that quality can be assured.

Students' evaluation of teaching is important to the scientific development of pedagogy. It is a student's right to meaningfully criticize the learning experience. Teachers will require their input in order to sharpen communication skills and become more effective content developers. While policy initiatives and strategic plans are in place and speak to this perspective, it is imperative that all members of the institution participate fully and equally.

[The student must feel welcomed, wanted and empowered in all areas of the environment]

Rising Remand

The 1990s witnessed what has been described as a revolution in the demand for higher education in the English-speaking subregion. The knowledge-driven third millennium has already impacted public consciousness in a way that should surprise no one with an awareness of the enormous importance attached to education in the people's flight from empire, and, indeed, long before.

UWI, described by Rex Nettleford as West Indians' greatest gift to themselves, has good reason to believe that it represents value for money. But it is also painfully aware that in its present institutional design cannot effectively meet the mass demand for higher education and training. The strategic response of the early 1990s to develop a tertiary institutional network, in which UWI is articulated with regional community colleges and other institutions in order to deliver cost-effective mass education, has run its course.

At the centre of this revolution in demand is the growing perception among young West Indians that access to higher education is the only reliable vehicle on which to travel in these turbulent, highly competitive postcolonial times.

[The strategic response of the early 1990s to develop a tertiary institutional network ... has run its course]

[Access to higher education is the only reliable vehicle on which to travel in these turbulent, highly competitive postcolonial times]

Expanding Capacity

Community colleges, polytechnics, at least one other national university (University of Technology, Jamaica) and a host of other higher education institutions have sprung up where formally only UWI offered the main illumination. This is all good and well. UWI has been empowered by the regional call to partner dozens of national institutions in meeting the academic and training needs of increasingly anxious communities.

The paradigm of an integrated network of national education institutions delivering higher education, however, is also shaped by the effective entry and, more importantly, the proliferation of non-national universities operating within the catchment. On the surface, the evidence seems clear. There is a perceived market for the product of these foreign institutions and in an age of educational liberalization, arrangements have been made for supply to meet demand. The thinking on the part of these non-regional universities is that the regional university system is

[UWI has been empowered by the regional call to partner dozens of national institutions]

ineffective with regard to community needs and that there is capacity to build with the stones UWI cannot accommodate.

✥ More Options

Beneath the surface, however, it is possible to discern other considerations. Some of these relate to how best to deliver a range and variety of educational services to a region willing to invest. Potential students of the non-national university system, excluded on grounds of programme unavailability and inflexibility, unresponsive matriculation regulations, and sheer physical incapacity, are seeking in large numbers access to providers who represent themselves as more protective and pertinent.

This development builds upon a well-established tradition of access to British higher education programmes by traditional correspondence modalities. What is new about their presence is that new information and communications technologies have allowed foreign-based institutions to migrate and engage directly with Caribbean students in their community.

✥ "Foreign" Universities

The message promoted by these non-national institutions is that by necessity they have to be more student friendly and supportive in non-traditional ways than UWI, and that this can be achieved. Their mass media advertisements speak to the use of advanced educational strategies and pedagogies that represent idealized learning environments.

Furthermore, an implication of their marketing statements is that they take on board students excluded by UWI, and they are fashioning a human resource strategy for the host society that is compelling and sound. Gradually, political leaders and other principal stakeholders of UWI throughout the region are making public statements of a positive comparative nature, the effect of which is to empower these institutions and legitimize them at the highest level.

Students and alumni of non-national institutions have been encouraged to speak about the creative solutions they found in programmes offered. In most cases, the tendency is for students and graduates to endorse statements made by some political leaders who perceive that a greater national interest is being served by their presence.

[There is capacity to build with the stones UWI has refused]

[The message promoted by these non-national institutions is that by necessity they have to be more student friendly]

✥ Doubts about Quality

The truth of the matter is that there is considerable unevenness in the quality and pertinence of programmes offered by these non-national universities. This suggests, therefore, the need to be cautious and detailed in any assignment of their effectiveness and the nature of their engagement. In some instances, programmes are comparable with what is expected of an internationally reputable institution, but in more cases there are disturbing signs that they represent inferior pedagogical interventions.

The issue of quality in higher education delivery, then, is a complex one that relies heavily upon notions about relevance. Only in cases where the programmes are designed specifically to meet community needs are they considered pertinent – a critical component in most concepts of quality.

It is possible, unfortunately, to discern cases where offshore universities have developed sound programmes for their overseas core students but offer weak and irrelevant options to locals as part of their strategy to secure a firm footing within the community. This is not the intention in all circumstances, but it is a consequence of the fact that the programme offered to locals is not part of the institution's known competence, pedagogical experience and stated intellectual mission.

The danger posed by these institutions in this circumstance is clear: the credibility of the core discipline is used as cover for "politically" inspired offerings in other areas. In conditions such as this local students are exploited in the worst possible fashion and offshore students are cast in the role of privileged outsiders in a dichotomous relationship that subverts the integrity of the institution's academic culture.

Quality and Development

Caribbean students, therefore, may require a measure of protection with respect to the neoliberal trend that has refashioned the higher education market via the globalization of programme delivery. While the concept of "choice" must be converted into a practical reality, it would be regressive to facilitate the emergence of inferior options that can only damage the long-term viability of the educational infrastructure.

Mindfulness is therefore to be recommended. The trend towards rapid growth has created a degree of chaos and unevenness within the

[There is considerable unevenness in the quality and pertinence of programmes offered by these non-national universities]

[There are disturbing signs that they represent inferior pedagogical interventions]

[The programme offered to locals is not part of the institution's known competence]

[Offshore students are cast in the role of privileged outsiders]

higher education sector. Orderly planning and rational expansion is preferred, of course, though it is not always possible. Certainly it does not follow that more is better; however, less can hardly be defended or admired.

In all these developments UWI has to take the strategic leadership in both diffusing notions of an uncaring educational national/regional sector and in the demonstration of creative responsiveness. A student-centred education sector must be promoted as the ideal, and all efforts must go towards its full realization.

The "Learning" Response

For the Caribbean community, the hard facts of globalization must be confronted with confidence and commitment. The first reality we must deal with is that sustainable development is directly an expression of the knowledge efficiency of the nation. Only communities that are aggressively engaging of higher education will secure a satisfactory living standard for their members. In the learning society of the near future all citizens will be required to access higher education if they wish to make a meaningful contribution to national development. In effect, what this means is that all Caribbean people will have to be prepared for and by a new education culture.

The government and people of Singapore have taken the lead once again with respect to this reality. What is now being called the New Singapore Model is not only about the macroeconomic policies that promoted the industrialization of the 1960s. It is a new set of perspectives on the role of higher education in the creation of a "high touch", creative and flexible mentality that is considered the core variable in development. The generation of new forms of knowledge and the growth of a civic society that reflects "high intelligence" in social action are the objectives of the new development strategy.

✥ *Quality and Capacity*

The social partners to public management in Singapore have declared that by the year 2020 it will be the "smartest" island on earth. By this they mean it will be a "learning" society dedicated to the maximization of the potential of all citizens by means of open access to higher education. The declaration of a policy of higher education for all is already

[The concept of "choice" must be converted to a practical reality]

[A student-centred education sector must be promoted as the ideal, and all efforts must go towards its full realization]

[Sustainable development is directly an expression of the knowledge efficiency of the nation]

being enforced aggressively. The bus driver is directed to enrol in a programme at the local university on environment and heritage, for example, and all jobs are linked to a process of educational training.

Open access and state-promoted engagement with respect to higher education is therefore the active vision of all institutional leaders who publicly declare the superiority of the "educated" society, the only kind they say that will be viable in the years ahead. They have redefined the notion of development by locating relevant education of the centre of the meaning of citizenship and nationhood.

UWI is well placed to assist the Caribbean in the formulation and implementation of such a compelling vision. Already the region is advancing along this road. There is a mature education culture and citizens value highly the importance of access to educational opportunities. The policy, however, has to move to the next level: tertiary education for all.

✤ Mature Students and Flexibility

The Board for Undergraduate Studies, which has responsibility for admission policies for UWI, recently revised the entry requirements in order to facilitate mass access for the creation of the "learning society". Mature persons, now defined as individuals over the age of 21 years, who do not possess the traditional entry requirements can be admitted into many programmes on the basis of their life experiences and aptitude. This policy shift has brought UWI in line with the most progressive higher education institutions. All citizens, particularly those from families without a background in higher education, should now locate a university experience within their life plan.

Flexible Systems

The English-speaking subregion is most challenged in regard to flexibility. There is little time for slow movement or blind belief in traditional methods of engaging and accessing the tertiary sector. The subregion has the lowest higher education enrolment ratios in the hemisphere, but it has one of the most dynamic civilizations on the planet. The thirst for education and the potential of the region are enormous. Not to effectively plan the issue of educational development is to subvert its future.

[The declaration of a policy of higher education for all is already being enforced aggressively]

[Mature persons, now defined as individuals over the age of 21 years, who do not possess the traditional entry requirements can be admitted into many programmes on the basis of their life experiences and aptitude]

[The subregion has ... one of the most dynamic civilizations on the planrt]

CARICOM heads of government have called for movement to at least 15 per cent enrolment of the cohort 18 to 30 years by 2005. To reach this target will be a struggle, even though it will be woefully insufficient as far as impacting development is concerned.

Caribbean Lags Behind

The Spanish-speaking Caribbean subregion is racing to reach Latin American enrolment ratios, and it is doing well. In some parts of Asia, where economic growth is impressive and social transformation spectacular, enrolment ratios are in excess of 60 per cent.

The challenge for the Caribbean is to effect, in the first instance, an attitudinal transformation. That is, we must popularize the idea, by rooting it in the realm of common sense, that without tertiary education the citizen will be largely dysfunctional in the changed global circumstance.

There has been some progress in this regard, and this progress is reflected in the rapidly growing demand witnessed in the last decade. But while it is necessary to continue pushing in this direction there must be a corresponding determination to expand capacity within the sector. Already a significant part of the problem faced is that demand is rapidly outstripping capacity, resulting in chaos and structural distortions within the sector.

Uneven Demand

UWI cannot cope with the demand in many disciplinary areas. The professional faculties – law, engineering and medicine – cannot offer places to all those who qualify and who are sought after by universities in North America especially. The Faculty of Social Sciences, which currently accounts for half of the students at UWI, is congested and has had ceilings placed on enrolment. The humanities will soon reach a similar point.

The sciences and technologies faculties continue to have unfilled capacities, largely because of another serious problem: the inability of the pre-university sector to supply the output required to feed these faculties. Only the radical transformation of science education in the school system can reverse this disturbing trend. There is much urgency in this

[The challenge for the Caribbean is to effect, in the first instance, an attitudinal transformation]

[Demand is rapidly outstripping capacity, resulting in chaos and structural distortions within the sector]

[Only the radical transformation of science education in the school system can reverse this disturbing trend]

regard because much of the new knowledge that is driving growth and development in the globalized sectors is rooted within the disciplines defined as science and technology related.

Planning for the Future

Other universities, many of them non-national with agendas not focused on regional development, are flooding in to generate wealth by engaging the demand. We need greater clarity on how to plan for the future. The options are many: movement to online delivery, the creation of more independent national university colleges from the existing community colleges, distance education and the liberalization of the sector are all on the agenda. What is required is a regional strategic response that will bring order and a sense of rational planning to the issue. The Association of Tertiary Level Institutions (ACTI) has started. It must push forward.

Clearly the time has come for a Caribbean commission on higher education. The education revolution that is needed is about the recreation of an entirely new mentality. In this regard, the future of Caribbean civilization is at stake, and educators must approach the challenge with a sense of the gravity implied.

[We need greater clarity on how to plan for the future]

[Clearly the time has come for a Caribbean commission on higher education]

4 New Challenges
E-Learning and Student Centredness

There is global consensus that the concepts of student friendliness and student centredness (not one and the same thing) are critical to an understanding of what "quality" is within academic environments. The former concept speaks to the removal of intimidatory elements within academic relations and the treatment of students as future colleagues, while the latter is a value system in which students are considered the main reason for an institution being in the education business.

What Students Want

[The concept of student friendliness and student centredness . . . are critical to an understanding of "quality"]

Research carried out among students in universities the world over indicates that there are ten general areas of concern:

1. Academic advising
2. Campus life
3. Campus support systems
4. Concern for the individual
5. Instructional effectiveness
6. Recruitment and financial aid
7. Registration effectiveness
8. Safety and security
9. Service excellence
10. Staff relations

These issues now dominate the politics of academic institutions and are determining, in large measure, their national and international standing.

In the context of UWI, there is a considerable challenge to implement this shared vision in a way that indicates deep conviction. In recent years there has been much movement along this path within campuses and beyond, but the overall result has been uneven and falls short of being impressive. While the commitment to change is there, at all levels of the academy, persistent inertia and conservative thinking remain important and determining forces.

Quality Is an Experience

The future of UWI as a centre of excellence will be determined by the extent to which there is public recognition of success. External stakeholders are insisting that students and graduates should experience and be placed in a position to report that the quality of day-to-day life within the learning community is consistent with this consensus.

Since the 1980s, when the massification of the undergraduate environment kicked into high gear, a crisis has been recognized with respect to students' overall relations within the academy. The indicative results of graduate exit polls and alumni surveys have shown that a primary concern of students remains the extent to which they feel alienated and unsupported within the expanded demographic reality.

The tension that exists between the traditional and modern approach has found expression at all levels of the environment, in academic relations as well as administrative management. It is driven by the students' belief that there is no systematic attempt to engage their understanding of the problem, and this circumstance deepens their perception of themselves as second-class stakeholders.

Intimacy

Against this background, students continue to call for an academic environment that is textured by systematic consultation and intimacy. In general, their demand is for the redesign of regulatory structures in faculties and central management, and the wholehearted application of the principle that students are the core purpose for the university's existence. That is, they want abolished the legacies of the traditional approach in which students are seen as a transient community to be firmly regulated and bureaucratically suppressed.

New Challenges: E-Learning and Student Centredness

[They want abolished the legacies of the traditional approach in which students are seen as a transient community to be firmly regulated]

While students accept that significant positive changes have been made along these lines in recent years, their overall assessment is that traditional attitudes, some of them connected to social opinions about "young" people in general, remain an inhibiting factor in the transition to a student-centred culture.

Changing Expectations

The student cohort has aged considerably in the last decade. The average age of campus-based students is in excess of 21 years and is rising. UWI, then, is no longer a space dominated by teenagers. It is a mature adult environment in which the typical student is a working parent rather than a recent school-leaver.

[The average age of campus-based students is in excess of 21 years]

The extent to which teachers have adjusted their social and academic relations to accommodate this changed circumstance of the student cohort is subject to debate. It is significant, though, that mature adults in the student body have shown a greater inclination to raise concerns, particularly with respect to inflexibility in the application of regulations governing access to programmes and the intimidatory network of bureaucratic procedures.

It is possible to discern those tensions within the academic community that originate within the wider society. But the many structural changes that have taken place within the academy in recent years have not been as effectively managed as the situation demanded. The impact of tuition fees on student attitudes, for example, is a matter that still requires full scientific study. The academy would benefit by way of more effective policy implementation.

Stresses and Tensions

[The impact of tuition fees on student attitudes, for example, is a matter that still requires elaborate scientific study]

Student exposure to online educational packages offered by competing higher education institutions has enabled a comparative framework within which programme delivery at UWI, high academic standard not withstanding, is seen as being high stress and low touch. In addition, the perception of excessive bureaucracy in student management systems is associated with the traditional top-down approach and its corresponding mentality.

Students, it should be noted, have tended to show sensitivity to the challenges facing their teachers, such as excessive teaching hours, unsatis-

[Programme delivery at UWI, high academic standard not withstanding, is seen as being high stress and low touch]

factory salaries, and overcrowded and ill-equipped facilities. As such, their expectation is that teachers will champion their concern for greater administrative flexibility, high-touch social services and general moral support.

The challenge is on and will be waged at all levels of academic relations and within the wider society. The effective promotion of human resource development as part of national growth strategies will depend on the extent to which universities are able to create a welcoming community for students.

Quality as a Tool for Development

The reform campaign to relocate students at the centre of institutional learning cultures has assumed proportions much larger than requirements specific to higher education planning. It is a campaign waged in order to facilitate the cultural regeneration of Caribbean society. The outcome will tell us all that is needed to know about the region's potential for transformation and development.

[The vision and operational systems of UWI will necessitate a new management culture]

The vision and operational systems of UWI will necessitate a new management culture. This culture should promote and measure what is quality education through modalities of student evaluation and reporting. The impact of any shortfall in such strategic thinking and acting upon the landscape of student life will be discernible. It will be here, on this landscape, that the battle to secure and protect the future of UWI, in an age of higher education liberation and globalization, will be fought and won.

A Quality Graduate

Over 75 per cent of students at UWI are undergraduates and, as such, they constitute its heartland. Stakeholders have called for an undergraduate programme that is expansive but relevant, high quality but cost effective, and interdisciplinary. It suggested that the programmes should promote the overall development of the student as an effective citizen and produce a graduate who is educated to be creative in the rapidly changing circumstances of the region. Importantly, it demanded that students should experience academic and social growth in an environment that is friendly and crafted around their needs.

[Stakeholders have called for an undergraduate programme that is expansive but relevant, high quality but cost effective, and interdisciplinary]

[Students should experience academic and social growth in an environment that is friendly and crafted around their needs]

However, the sum of achievements can best be described as disturbingly uneven. This assessment is based upon data generated by the UWI quality assurance reviews of a range of academic disciplines, conducted under the guidelines of the Office of the Board for Undergraduate Studies. The reports of the reviews have consistently stated the following:

- The quality of UWI's undergraduate programmes is high and internationally competitive.
- There is an urgent need for UWI to become more student friendly in its administrative procedures and their management.
- There is inadequate use being made of opportunities for feedback to students, particularly regarding the examination system, which appears in some cases to have become excessive.
- There is need for increased student access to new information and communications technologies.
- High academic standards notwithstanding, much greater connectivity and sensitivity to stakeholders' expectations are required in order to promote relevance, which is a core criterion in quality measurement.

The architecture and objectives of management thinking and action should be viewed within this context and against this background.

Undergraduate Studies and Development

[The global industrialization of higher education in the twenty-first century will constitute the primary force driving sustainable development]

The global industrialization of higher education in the twenty-first century will constitute the primary force driving sustainable development. A new education paradigm is rapidly evolving, in which institutions of higher education such as UWI must invest much greater thought and action in being student centred. This investment is the only way that their wider their role as international centres of excellence and engines of national development can be attained.

This deeply transforming process is fashioned by two inescapable forces: one is the growing social awareness of students about higher education as a civil right and the attendant demand of citizens, in general, for inclusion in the benefits of development. The other relates to the knowledge revolution, which is driven by the new information and communications technologies. The background to these changes is the politically compelled vision of education as a popular, participatory experience of lifelong learning. Collectively, these forces have shattered traditionally elitist concepts and are aggressively democratizing access to university-based knowledge as a civil right with enormous development potential.

New Information and Communications Technologies

The exposure of the Caribbean higher education sector by technical and methodological solutions emanating from the new information and communications technologies has enormous implications for how UWI students are perceived and treated. The advent of asynchronous learning, for example, has the potential to liberate the learning environment from the traditional time and space constraints and to respond to the direct needs of students.

Resources must be secured to enable faculties to embrace the new learning and teaching culture of student centredness while expanding undergraduate capacity at lower per capita costs. An immediate objective should be to radically improve efficiency and reduce per capita costs of delivering student-centred undergraduate studies as a strategy to mobilize human capital for development.

UWI has have found itself occupying both sides of a debate on the role of new information and communications technologies in the learning environment. The insistence that UWI should provide the lead in facilitating the new learning culture, with all its electronic modalities, seems reasonable enough. But in Caribbean societies universities are not positioned to provide leadership and are in fact being dragged and pushed into the information age by other knowledge centres that surround them.

Policy on Education Technology

UWI has made a policy commitment to advance the development of the electronic teaching and learning culture. Many of its faculties are providing technical and conceptual services to other institutions. There remains, however, considerable inertia within their own environment to the transformation of traditional teaching modalities. In some instances, the reality of scarce resources provides a reasonable rationalization, but there is evidence that suggests other explanations.

[The new information and communications technologies have enormous implications for how UWI students are perceived and treated]

[Resources must be secured to enable faculties to embrace the new learning and teaching culture]

[UWI has made a policy commitment to advance the development of the electronic teaching and learning culture]

It is clear that teachers within UWI have not yet been persuaded in large enough numbers that the new information and communications technologies will enhance the teaching and learning process in ways that justify costs and training. This perception varies across faculties, producing an uneven terrain. But in general, there is at best slow preparation that could lead to a consensus around the point that a quality education product now requires intense engagement with the new information and communications technologies.

✥ Quality and Technology

Private sector stakeholders, however, have already reached this stage. Their view is that a quality degree programme can only be assured within the context of the new teaching and learning environments. That is, a graduate who is not proficient in the effective manipulation of electronic learning tools and technologies will not be competitive in the workplace, and would have received an education that is short on relevance.

Preparing the student with a relevant education, then, requires the fullest exposure to the new information and communications technologies. Quality cannot be assured outside of these pedagogical considerations. Graduates who are illiterate with respect to the electronic culture will not be a credit to any aspect of the national development agenda.

This publication deals with some of the challenges that will be encountered in the transition from a traditional teaching and learning environment to an electronic learning culture. The focus is upon those challenges posed to members of teaching and administrative staff, resource producers, and the students. UWI is seen as poised to make the grand leap, and it is in the process of working out anticipated difficulties. While the enthusiasm is less than universal, the will in significant sections of the community is seen as sufficient to take the entire system forward with balance and care.

[A quality degree programme can only be assured within the context of the new teaching and learning environments]

[A relevant education, then, requires the fullest exposure to the new information and communications technologies]

The Productivity Factor

Information technologies idealize productivity as a principal objective. That is, how to do it better, quicker and cheaper. These three factors — quality, time and cost — are set apart as signposts that guide and inform journeys to excellence.

Cutting-edge education technologies, especially, are discussed in this way, and the case for their use is made within universities with an even greater intensity. This is so because issues of costs and "quality" in higher education, at a time of diminishing resources available to the sector, have generated a feverish response in the academic environments within which all universities have to function effectively.

The discourse strikes at the core of UWI's sense of its role and contribution. As an international institution UWI is sensitive to global trends. Its input as a development force are critical. Located as it is in a region whose economies are struggling to generate surpluses also serves to assure its operations receive intense stakeholder scrutiny. Its engagement in the education technology debate, therefore, should tell us a great deal about its preparedness to fulfil its mandate.

[As an international institution UWI is sensitive to global trends]

Building Intimacy

There are related considerations that confront UWI in regard to the education technology debate. One is the matter of building intimacy in the learning process. Another is the role of technology in enhancing productivity in the student-teacher relationship. Intimacy, in UWI's case, relates to two distinct processes within the educational environment.

The first of these is the use of education technologies in the harnessing and fashioning of a Caribbean education village. UWI was set up as an engine to drive this process by creating a specific kind of popular consciousness that would foster the integration agenda.

Eric Williams's statement in relation to the collapse of the Federation, "Let no man put together what God has put asunder", remains the challenge faced by UWI: to defy God, so to speak, as Williams would have it, and manufacture from our diversity a oneness of purpose and vision.

[UWI was set up as an engine to drive this process by creating a specific kind of popular consciousness that would foster the integration agenda]

✣ Distance Education

To date, considerable effort has been made in distance education at UWI. In terms of creating the infrastructure for the Caribbean education village, significant advances have been recorded. There is in place a broad-based platform that can enable the achievement of this objective. The requirement is for the exercise to attain the level of quality expected by stakeholders – student-users especially.

[A major challenge is to build, bottom up, a quality assurance process]

A major challenge is to build, bottom up, a quality assurance process that will facilitate operations and development of the distance education service. Another is to complement distance learning with online teaching and learning capability in order to fashion a self-instructional education culture that is consistent with the logic and rhythm of the Information Age.

A second challenge is to build greater intimacy within the educational process at UWI. This is no less challenging than the first. Both concern the use of educational technologies to strengthen bonds between students and teachers so as to maximize learning productivity and transform notions of how students learn and what is the role of the teacher in knowledge creation and dissemination.

Diffusing the Negatives

With regard to the challenges above, UWI is at the wicket and, while not batting with the level of comfort and ease that many would like, it is adding to the total of runs and the team is making progress. In many universities in the developed countries negative results are being registered because too many teachers have become technophiles, marvelling at the technologies and using these new technologies simply because they are there. At UWI, however, some teachers are still technophobes, not keen to engage the usefulness of the technologies in the teaching exercise. The balance, of course, is what is desired in most universities.

[In many universities in the developed countries negative results are being registered because too many teachers have become technophiles ...At UWI, however, some teachers are still technophobes]

There are special ways that UWI can achieve an effective and creative sense of intimacy in the development of the electronic-learning classroom for undergraduate teaching. It has already established a formidable reputation as a teaching institution. The UWI lecturer is a global leader and is distinguished for effectiveness in voice communications and course design, lecturing to large groups, and conducting intensive discourse in small group seminars.

[The UWI lecturer is a global leader and is distinguished for effectiveness in voice communications and course design]

It is their belief in, and commitment to, the effectiveness of these modalities that now constitute a source of inertia in building the electronic learning capability. This inevitability has also been demonstrated by several cases in other respected universities. A period of cultural preparation for the electronic classroom is clearly required. But there is little time, and the adjustment process has to be intensive.

Protecting Orality

UWI's challenge, then, is how to protect the enormous oral communications capital of its faculty, as far as teaching is concerned, from the fall-out associated with the transformation to electronic classroom modalities. It is for teachers to begin by seeing electronic technologies not as substitutes and alternatives but as extensions of themselves. The faculty centredness of UWI and the suspicions surrounding electronic modes of teaching may well serve as important forces in achieving a balanced perspective.

Electronic technologies will not in themselves produce an excellent lecturer or seminar facilitator. It is for colleagues to identify, within the quality assurance discourse, their problems in the teacher-student exchange and see how best electronic technologies may assist in solving them. In exactly the same way that a lecturer might be a poor oral communicator he or she could also maintain that reputation by using electronic technologies. That is, dull interactions within traditional modalities can also be maintained by unimaginative high-tech presentations.

All forms of teaching are about stimulating the imagination of students. This can be done in many modes. Computerized technology is just one, but it is the great enabler, and, given its ability to combine sound, real and graphic images, and to interface the real and virtual, its power to stimulate is enormous. However, it should always be people centred, which makes the imagination of the teacher the key force within the configuration. High-tech, then, does not make the presentation complex or guarantee that students reflect; rather, it is the intellect of the tutor that creates these worlds within which students journey.

⁕ Problem-Solving Electronically

Alan Kay of Apple Computers was precise when he said, "Any problem the schools cannot solve without computers, they cannot solve with them." UWI faculty, then, must know exactly the limits of low-tech teaching, the problems it presents within the information age and what must be done to maintain quality teaching under the changed circumstances. There is no doubt that mass enrolment and high-tech expectations have changed UWI's academic environments. What is on the agenda is its strategic response in order to maintain quality.

[Electronic technologies will not in themselves produce an excellent lecturer or seminar facilitator]

[All forms of teaching are about stimulating the imagination of students]

[It is the intellect of the tutor that creates these worlds within which students journey]

The challenge is to find a UWI approach that combines traditional language skills and electronic technologies. The excellence of many UWI teachers in the classical art of oratory must not be sacrificed. The "voice" has stimulated UWI students to excellence from the beginning, and should have a central role to play in the new dispensation.

Students whose imaginations are not stimulated will not disappear simply by developing the electronic classroom. A PowerPoint delivery, no matter how skilful, without a compelling concept and a powerful message content does not add value. An online capacity without creative and relevant content design adds no value. Quality begins with the imagination and ends with intellectual improvement. Electronic technology can enable us to do this better, clearer and faster, but it cannot do it in itself, by itself. Excellence in both oral and electronic modalities, then, should be our ideal.

[Mass enrolment and high-tech expectations have changed UWI's academic environments]

[The excellence of many UWI teachers in the classical art of oratory must not be sacrificed]

[Quality begins with the imagination and ends with intellectual improvement]

✣ What Can Be Done

The purpose of the Instructional Development Units on the campuses is to enable teachers to use graphic presentation software such as Microsoft PowerPoint, the World Wide Web, e-mail, chat rooms, interactive videos and electronic bulletin boards as extensions of their creative imaginations and thought processes, while using the mastery of language as the binding force. This way, the introduction of new information and communications technologies does not replace in the classroom the intellectual impact of the teacher. The objective of creating an appropriate asynchronous teaching and learning culture can still be achieved.

Insistence upon the need for a culturally relevant electronic-learning environment, though, cannot be overstated. But if development discourse has taught us anything, it is that technologies must connect to the imagination and cultural reflexes of a people in order to be productive. The key words have to be, "Know your culture." Unless this is done within the context of UWI, electronic technologies will enhance cultural alienation rather than intellectual intimacy within the classroom. The damage will be considerable if such an error is made. Doing it right at the outset, on the other hand, will strengthen UWI in ways that stakeholders expect.

✥ The Effective Communicator

Each UWI faculty member should be trained in order to engage students with the latest electronic technologies as well as in the traditional art of oratory. The reason for this is simple: no university today can risk producing students who are not versatile in e-learning technologies. If they do, programmes will have no "quality". A graduate without these capabilities would not have had a quality education as far as world opinion is concerned. To expose students to the risk of having their degrees questioned and negated could be interpreted as irresponsibility on the part of an institution. The process of preparation at UWI, then, has to be advanced along the lines already set out and deepened with respect to the issue of cultural relevance.

✥ Interactive Teaching

Student's expectation of higher education, furthermore, is that intimacy in staff-student exchange within the learning environment should be a norm. The paradigm now calls for a blurring of the boundaries between student and staff. Interactive teaching creates learning opportunities for both parties. Hierarchy in relations is being flattened and mutualism is emerging as a desired condition. Learning has become a two-way, intergenerational discourse that is continual. Electronic technologies can serve to revolutionize data content and delivery parameters.

UWI must continue to make significant advances within the arena of electronic learning and teaching. The quality graduate, revolutionary increases in enrolment, institutional effectiveness and efficiency, lower per capita costs, and pedagogical relevance can only be attained and maintained by speedy and balanced movement across this frontier. Such a journey will require that much baggage be left behind

The principal challenge is to create and manage a creative, cost-effective teaching and learning culture for students. This expectation should provoke the entire tertiary education sector in many ways. UWI, in particular, is expected to increase public understanding of the issues involved and provide educational strategies to raise awareness and solve problems Furthermore, UWI is expected, by its own conduct, to provide leadership by generating best practices within its stakeholder community.

[Technologies must connect to the imagination and cultural reflexes of a people in order to be productive]

[No university today can risk producing students who are not versatile in e-learning technologies]

[Interactive teaching creates learning opportunities for both parties]

[UWI, in particular, is expected to increase public understanding of the issues]

Student Preparation

The community of scholars at UWI is mandated to develop innovative, multidisciplinary and pertinent undergraduate programmes. All curricula should locate the key messages of education within the complex notion of sustainable development for coming generations. In preparing to meet the evolving needs of society, UWI will be required to combine teaching and training that stimulate students to pursue and develop new knowledge.

UWI has long taken the first step. It is cognizant of its identity as the principal knowledge centre within the subregion. It is also aware that it is not just a teaching and training academy but a place of critical thinking, social reflection and scientific development. UWI's programme development, pedagogical visions and methods of teaching and training are undergoing constant redesign, driven by the quality discourse within the education sector. The preparation of students for citizenship, employability and job security in a rapidly changing society is at the core of UWI's understanding of its role in sustainable development.

❖ The Graduate Advantage

A UWI undergraduate degree impacts positively on the life experiences of its holder. It raises wages and productivity and enhances the quality of civil society. A graduate can reasonably expect to earn 50 per cent more than a non-graduate within the short term and 100 per cent more in the medium to long term.

The macroeconomic impact of the undergraduate degree is therefore strong. Just as individuals with better education tend to succeed more in the labour market, so economies with higher undergraduate enrolment rates appear to be more dynamic, competitive in global markets and successful in terms of higher income per capita. The purpose of the undergraduate degree, therefore, is to:

- unlock human potential at all levels of society, helping talented people to gain advanced training, whatever their social background and sex;
- create a pool of highly trained individuals that exceeds a critical size and becomes a key national resource;
- address topics whose long-term value to society is thought to exceed their current value;

[UWI will be required to combine teaching and training that stimulate students to pursue and develop new knowledge]

[The preparation of students for citizenship, employability and job security in a rapidly changing society is at the core of UWI's understanding of its role in sustainable development]

[The macroeconomic impact of the undergraduate degree is therefore strong]

- provide the space for the free, open and critical discussion of ideas in order to foster the creation of shared values; and
- facilitate access to postgraduate training while enhancing the research capability of the society.

Growing Capacity

The proposal to expand the range and content of on-site and virtual delivery in the undergraduate programme hinges on two major concerns: increased levels of resources and improved efficiency in resource use. A larger and more diversified resource base is needed for:

- improving the educational infrastructure, especially computer and Internet access in developing the electronic teaching and learning environment (this includes libraries and other forms of data storage systems);
- development and implementation of new academic programmes and curricula, including the expansion of general education;
- intellectual motivation and training of teaching staff;
- conducting more and better science education, both basic and applied science education; and
- focusing on social capital development in the areas of health, social relations, citizenship and a culture of peace.

There is also a strong tradition within our catchment community that a university undergraduate education should transcend cognitive and intellectual development, and that it should use curricula (the teaching and learning environment) and experience to develop the character, autonomy and maturity of the whole person. That is, it should target the inner resource potential of the individual student. For this reason, a creative tension should fashion the relationships between the concepts of specialization and generalization within the curriculum of the undergraduate landscape.

[University undergraduate education should transcend cognitive and intellectual development]

Enrolment and Cohort Demographics

The undergraduate student population increased from 18,001 in academic year 1997/98 to 19,320 at the beginning of academic year

1999/2000. During this period the undergraduate population represented between 82 per cent and 86 per cent of the total on- and off-campus student registration. The number of full-time students continues to be about twice the number of part-time students.

The UWI Strategic Plan, 1997–2002, called for total student enrolment to increase by an average of 1,000 full-time equivalents (FTEs) each year. The target is an FTE enrolment of 21,000 students at the end of the five-year period. The actual yearly increase for 1998/99 and 1999/2000 has fallen short of projected enrolment. At the Cave Hill campus FTE enrolment stands at 2,971, 7 per cent above the target of 2,780 for the 1999/2000 academic year; Mona and St Augustine campuses experienced growth but felt short of projected targets.

An important objective set out in the Strategic Plan is to increase in absolute and relative terms FTE undergraduate enrolment in science and technology disciplines, broadly defined. This reflects the critical need to strengthen and expand these aspects of popular culture. Enhancing the science sensibility within mass society should remain a core objective of UWI, and a strong undergraduate programme in the sciences is the means to this end. It is stipulated in the 1997–2002 strategic plan that 50 per cent of the FTE enrolment should be in the faculties that embrace agriculture, natural sciences, pure and applied sciences, engineering and medicine by 2002.

[Enhancing the science sensibility within mass society should remain a core objective of UWI]

❖ Quality and Quantity

In the 1998/99 academic year undergraduate FTE enrolment in the sciences stood at 39 per cent with an upward trend identified in the 1999/2000 year. With respect to the Faculty of Pure and Applied Sciences, though, the trend has been negative at the Mona campus where enrolment in this faculty fell by about 5 per cent to 1,211 in 1998/99. In 1999/2000 enrolment fell even lower to 1,194.

At the St Augustine campus, FTE enrolment, exclusive of the Faculty of Medical Sciences, increased from 4,367 students in 1996/97 to 4,858 in 1999/2000 in contrast to the projected level of 5,489 FTE students. Enrolment in the Faculty of Engineering is 12 per cent below target. In the Faculty of Agriculture and Natural Sciences enrolment is 27 per cent below target. Agriculture's FTE enrolment decreased from 366 students in 1996/97 to 285 in 1999/2000. Natural sciences experienced growth from 768 to 885 over the corresponding period. In the agriculture programme, the ten-year decline between 1989 and 1999 is from 454 FTEs to 331 FTEs.

At the Cave Hill campus, enrolment in the Faculty of Science and Technology increased from 665 to 693 between 1997/98 and 1998/99 (4 per cent) to 783 in 1999/2000 (11.4 per cent). The projection for 2000/2001 was 786. This achievement is driven by two important developments: (1) increased enrolment within tertiary level institutions in non-campus countries in UWI's courses, as well as the distance education programme, and (2) more flexible and innovative interdisciplinary programme offerings.

Another objective of the university is to reduce, in relative terms, enrolment in undergraduate programmes by increasing the number of postgraduate students to 20 per cent of the FTE enrolment by the end of 2002/2003.

Falling Science Enrolment

Science faculties continue to pose special challenges with respect to meeting enrolment targets. The Office of Special Initiatives has participated in various discussions and investigations seeking to understand the problems associated with deficit enrolment in these faculties. The severe limitations of science education in the region's pre-tertiary sectors constitute the overarching explanation. In the largest societies, Trinidad and Tobago and Jamaica, a growing preference for non-regional universities within the cohort serves to aggravate what could otherwise be a moderate enrolment performance.

[The region is suffering a substantial brain drain within the cohort and this is serving to subvert science education expectations]

The strategic decision to articulate science education provision in the secondary and non-university tertiary sectors to generate larger numbers of applicants has been partly successful. Benefits, however, have been nullified by the competitive ability of non-regional universities. They attract an increasing share of the cohort by offering generous funding packages, often to potential science and technology applicants, some of whom had already been accepted to UWI. In effect, the region is suffering a substantial brain drain within the cohort and this is serving to subvert science education expectations.

✥ Building the Science Culture

The introduction of a preliminary science programme within the Faculty of Pure and Applied Sciences at the Mona campus contributed towards increasing enrolment. Recognizing the inadequacy of science-teaching capability in the pre-university sector, the faculty took on the task of facilitating the academic upgrading of students for direct entry into science degree programmes. To date, this programme has had moderate success.

While it continues to be weakened by an unacceptable attrition rate, largely the result of student migration into higher profile programmes, including other science disciplines such as medicine, the faculty can take some satisfaction in the reasonable student performance measured by their rate of progression through courses.

✥ Science, Technology and Quality

The Faculty of Pure and Applied Sciences at Mona remains committed to the preliminary programme, albeit in a revised and more cost-effective format. Their proposal is to keep enrolment levels steady while working with tertiary level institutions to develop their capacity to enhance science teaching. A review undertaken by the faculty suggests that the elimination of the programme at this time would seriously undermine UWI's commitment to building an advanced science culture within the region.

Importance should be attached to the fact that the trend in student performance has been positive. With greater attention paid to pedagogical concerns in this programme, this trend can be enhanced in the short term. But even more important is that the preliminary science programme has proven a valuable foundation for students who have graduated with degrees, particularly in the life sciences.

[The preliminary science programme has proven a valuable foundation for students]

In the quest for greater efficiency and programme innovation for capacity building, the faculty has taken a rational path with respect to the preliminary science programme. While the faculty should continue to advance the effort to divest as much of the programme as possible to partners in the sector, it cannot deny the special development role of the programme at this moment.

Financial Challenges to Quality

Strategic planning seeks to promote creative responses to challenges posed by significant absolute increases in undergraduate enrolment within the context of diminishing financial support from the traditional sponsors: the regional governments. These governments have undertaken to ensure that by the year 2005, 15 per cent of the subregional age cohort will be enrolled in the tertiary sector, out of which UWI is expected to account for 6 per cent. The cohort enrolment level in 1997 stood at about 8 per cent – the lowest among hemispheric subgroups.

Within this context of rapidly increasing enrolment with less than matching financial resources from governments, concern exists with regard to the quality, pertinence and scope of the first degree. The issue of quality assurance focuses on matters such as the nature of teaching, the supportiveness of the learning environment, relevance and innovation in programmes, and the availability and standards of student amenities.

Quality Assurance Unit

The establishment of the Quality Assurance Unit within the Office of the Board for Undergraduate Studies in the 2001/2002 academic year has enabled UWI to approach quality reviews and audits of the undergraduate and postgraduate teaching and learning environment in a professional manner.

Importantly, the quality assurance process should be supported at a level that will also secure non-academic objectives within the academy. For example, stakeholders must be satisfied that the University is not paying lip-service to the concept of student centredness. An academic environment that is student centred will have the following non-academic characteristics:

1. Rules and regulations are conceived and designed to enhance the learning opportunities of students.

2. Rules and regulations are applied in a manner that is non-threatening of students and respectful of their status as the core reason for the university's existence.

[These governments have undertaken to ensure that by the year 2005, 15 per cent of the subregional age cohort will be enrolled in the tertiary sector]

[The issue of quality assurance focuses on matters such as the nature of teaching, the supportiveness of the learning environment, relevance and innovation in programmes]

3. Contact between students and the administrative machinery is hassle free and non-confrontational.

4. Students are seen and treated as future staff and therefore empowered with a sense of responsibility for the welfare of the academy.

5. Examination systems and procedures are designed to test rather than intimidate and physically exhaust. At present, the examination machinery is inefficient in its consumption of time and resources. Students are overexamined and teachers are stressed. The evidence suggests that more creative ways of testing are required throughout the entire system.

There will be a threat to quality in the academic culture of the undergraduate experience if these features are not in place and operational.

Countering Student Alienation

To counter the growing sense of student alienation and insufficient informal contact with teachers, it might be useful at this time to introduce the personal tutor system in all faculties and teaching units. This is an arrangement whereby each student is allocated a personal tutor within the faculty who functions as advisor and facilitator.

Students have consistently expressed a desire for better quality in their contact with teachers, as well as departmental and faculty leadership. The personal tutor system promotes collegiality and mutual access. It is a standard mechanism in most universities that seek to implement a student friendly culture.

Evidence indicates that stakeholders have cause to be concerned these and other matters. A regional employers' survey conducted by the Office of the Board for Undergraduate Studies suggests that while the work performance of students shows high standards of teaching that enable an effective grasp of regional problems and a commitment to solving them, there is the disturbing sign of inadequate training with respect to acquiring directly applicable industry skills. Also, the results of a graduates' survey conducted by the Office of the Board for Undergraduate Studies reinforce the point of student satisfaction with the teaching and learning experience at UWI but also indicate serious concerns about a lack of innovative programmes in the newer disciplinary areas.

[It might be useful at this time to introduce the personal tutor system in all faculties and teaching units]

[The personal tutor system promotes collegiality and mutual access]

[There is the disturbing sign of inadequate training with respect to acquiring directly applicable industry skills]

Countering Perceptions

A principal challenge for UWI, then, within the context of future strategic planning, is to turn around these perceptions and realities and ensure that all students have skills that are relevant, modern, and honed to the needs of the workplace and modern citizenship. Inadequate skills in oral and written communication in one or more non-national languages, ineffectual proficiency in computing and quantitative analysis, inadequate industry-based knowledge about the tourism sector, and insufficient exposure to e-markets continue to be high on the list of employers' concerns.

No student should graduate from UWI in 2007, the end of the next five-year planning cycle, without basic proficiency in a foreign language. In addition, new and innovative programmes should be developed in the disciplinary areas associated with the leading-edge sectors of the economy such as tourism, offshore finance and e-markets.

Relevance and Quality

The time lag between the shift from agricultural and manufacturing to international services as the engine of growth in most Caribbean economies and initiatives in undergraduate curriculum development at UWI is evidence of insufficient direct correspondence between macroeconomic policy changes and academic programmes. This circumstance should highlight that UWI should pay urgent attention to compulsory training in new information and communications technologies, foreign languages, and the new economic sectors within the undergraduate experience. The criterion of "pertinence" can be understood and accepted in this way as central to the quality discourse, in general, and specific to benchmarking exercises.

Notwithstanding the views expressed in both the employers' and the graduates' surveys, the global shift from an economic frame of reference to wider sociocultural themes in conceiving higher education policy for sustainable human development will impact upon UWI's undergraduate teaching and learning strategies.

Increasingly, greater attention is being given to the knowledge process of teaching and learning rather than narrow courses offering specific training. This movement has produced a conceptual rationale which facilitates the directing of undergraduate studies provision away from specialized skills to acquisition of more elastic, transferable skills.

✥ *The "Total" Student*

While economic objectives remain critical, citizens are concerned more than ever before with the effectiveness of civic institutions, human relations, public health and the environment. As a result, the undergraduate curriculum is pressed to confront cultural and social predicaments. Teaching and learning strategies to ensure the expansion of students' capacity for critical thinking, as opposed to specific training for direct employment, are gaining ground as important approaches to human resource preparation.

The introduction in 1998/99 of a menu of compulsory foundation courses in multidisciplinary pedagogical areas, for example, is evidence of this search for an intellectually generic student mentality. Within this context, a formal place should be found, and funded, within the undergraduate matrix for the Caribbean cultural studies as an interdisciplinary platform.

[Teaching and learning strategies to ensure the expansion of students' capacity for critical thinking ... are gaining ground as important approaches to human resource preparation]

Creative Thinking and Acting

UWI graduates are expected to be more creative in social living, flexible in attitudes towards work and adaptive in responses to the labour market. They are required to possess a broader portfolio of technical, social, cultural and personal skills.

The acquisition of technical expertise will not be diminished, but greater weight is now given to a wider range of personal competencies. One reason is that the increasing focus upon team and project approaches to problem solving and the widespread use of total quality methods of self-directed work have placed a premium on the acquisition of generic skills for citizenship and employability.

Success in achieving these policy objectives will determine if future generations of graduates will state that UWI was a crucial rite of passage in their development as citizens. This is a challenge for which UWI can only contemplate a positive outcome. In this regard, the cultivation in students of a sense of critical independent thought is necessary for enhancing healthy democracies.

[Graduates are expected to be more creative in social living, flexible in attitudes towards work and adaptive in responses to the labour market]

[The cultivation in students of a sense of critical independent thought is necessary for enhancing healthy democracies]

It is one way that young people can be equipped to examine and evaluate the complex realities they will encounter in life. Development begins with each citizen contributing to a vibrant culture by acquiring the "arts of living" through higher education.

In the Caribbean world, then, the undergraduate experience continues to be critical to establishing and maintaining the interconnections among education, work, lifestyle, identity and meaningful citizenship.

5 Open Access and Quality Issues

[There are no reliable tests for readiness and willingness]

[The only sure test for university preparedness is university]

[In today's complex world, a high school education is not sufficient]

There are no good predictors for university performance, nor are there any non-controversial standards for "success". The criteria used for entry in the United States – Scholastic Aptitude Test (SAT) scores, high school grade-point averages – are only self-fulfilling: they prove that people who do well on tests before they begin university tend to do well on tests in the university as well. There are no reliable tests for readiness and willingness, no computer-graded examinations to measure enthusiasm or creativity or intellectual curiosity. There is no way to tell which students are late bloomers. The only sure test for university preparedness is university.

In the Caribbean, access to UWI has been perceived as a main avenue for helping people achieve upward mobility. Many also argue that UWI plays a key role in realizing the ideals of a regional society. However, some critics of UWI have questioned the claim and say that it remains rigid by the very nature of acceptance policies.

Education Investment

Although it might appear contradictory, those who hold the view that equality of opportunity through education increases the chances of upward social mobility are often also those proponents of limited access. By contrast, the egalitarian view of open admission espouses that all – or at least nearly all – must be admitted to higher education and treated equally when they get there. It furthers the argument by suggesting that in today's complex world, a high school education is not sufficient for anyone.

Effective and meaningful participation in contemporary social, political and economic life demands the greater awareness and broader understanding that only universities can supply. From society's perspective, higher learning amounts to an investment promising better-informed citizens and more highly skilled workers. It is an expenditure no developing economy can afford to do without.

More people will be admitted to university given an acceptance of the ideal of mass higher education. Thus expanding higher education opportunities, widening the curricula, establishing new courses and programmes, and diversifying the approaches to teaching and learning are argued in the discourse of the massification of higher education. The presence of larger numbers of those students formerly discouraged from attending university supports this position.

Types of Universities

University matriculation and eligibility rules, academic standards and quality issues need not be antithetical to the debate over quantity. You can have it both ways: the academic achievements of the outstanding few are not undermined by the successes of the many. Both are possible and desirable. One observer, commenting on the coexistence of mediocrity and excellence on the campuses of elite universities such as Oxford and Cambridge, noted that they nurtured "agreeable and moneyed boneheads" alongside "the most brilliant intellects of the nation."

At times conservatism is disguised under metaphors of intellectual standards and "unqualified" students. For many persons, increasing access is associated with the lowering of academic standards. The discourse of selectivity and equity in access to higher education is constructed around political, economic, academic, institutional and personal contexts. The discourse concerns who can legitimately claim rights to publicly funded resources that potentially lead to enhanced lifetime status and earnings, and how selection and equity interact, particularly for adults. In the Caribbean the transformation from elitism to the massification of higher education continues to stir much controversy.

Access Instruments

A significant aspect of the debate is related to the qualification routes available. Academic traditionalists in the Caribbean place great emphasis upon the gold standard of Advanced level (A level) school certificates, which symbolize academic merit for many. These examinations are presented as being a neutral, fair and just selector of the suitable. Thus a

[Higher learning amounts to an investment promising better-informed citizens and more highly skilled workers]

[The academic achievements of the outstanding few are not undermined by the successes of the many]

[The discourse is about who can legitimately claim rights to publicly funded resources]

[For many persons, increasing access is associated with the lowering of standards]

normal, acceptable student is seen as one who has actually undergone a quite particular form of academic socialization, designed for 16- to 18-year-old students in high schools. On this basis, it is believed, a higher education institution can take for granted the preparation the individual has received and build on it.

For many years, universities in the United Kingdom relied on A levels to make all the decisions about who was to be admitted, although this has now changed considerably. UWI also followed this pattern for several decades. The academic quality of a department or institution is said to be reflected in the quality of its entrants and the selective nature of its entry criteria; such entry standards are believed to be unambiguously related to the quality of the output.

Selection Issues

It has been suggested that selectivity in admissions to universities in the United Kingdom began as a postwar phenomenon (and thus the current "reversal" to an open admissions policy would be nothing new). By the 1950s, the great demand for higher education meant that certain institutions had to be more selective and competitive in their admissions policies.

Extend that argument to UWI and it could be suggested that the demand for places at the undergraduate level necessarily makes the admission process a highly selective and competitive exercise. The long-held idea that higher education should be exclusive to an academic elite is still evident at UWI. Competition from other regional higher education institutions and offshore US universities has, however, begun to erode the belief that the region's best students will naturally apply to UWI. UWI should consider whether this may lead to the less able (by the traditional A level standards) filling its classrooms. A prominent academic recently remarked that it really does not matter what qualifications the students possess when they enter UWI; what matters is what UWI does to ensure its students then experience a high-quality education.

UWI's Challenge

The challenge facing UWI is the extent to which it can open its doors to more non-traditional students. It has to fashion a creative response to all those who wish to gain entry, while at the same time continuing to embrace the brightest of our high school graduates.

Opponents of wider access argue that UWI is already constrained by inadequate resources and facilities that could be further threatened if undergraduate enrolment figures increase. The role of the community and state colleges across the English-speaking Caribbean is being redesigned to meet the increased demands for education and training. The successes of the Antigua State College, Barbados Community College and the Sir Arthur Lewis Community College in St Lucia serve as models that could show us the way to extend access to higher education. These institutions now teach parts of UWI programmes, allowing easier and cheaper access for students in the respective countries and reducing pressure on the main campuses. Further efforts should be made to extend their contribution.

Increasing Enrolment

As noted previously, the English-speaking Caribbean lags behind Latin America, the United States and Canada in the percentage of its secondary school cohort that enrols in higher education institutions. The relative wealth of our neighbours is said to enable them to provide the resources to facilitate a steady increase in the number of places available in higher education institutions. The challenge in the United States, for instance, is how best to make colleges and universities more responsive to the needs of minorities, not whether expansion can occur, as the resources are available.

The Caribbean faces different dilemmas. The call to increase enrolment is not always matched with the offer of increased resources. There is rarely enough money to support the physical expansion required and also to maintain an adequate focus on the non-campus countries. Across the region educators and policy makers argue that primary and secondary education should be given priority. This is partly because they recognize that the most disadvantaged in the society do not benefit from expansion in higher education; the returns from investments in primary education seem more visible in poor societies. Additionally, a criticism in development discourse is that any social provision that benefits the few has to be viewed as a luxury.

[The challenge facing UWI is the extent to which it can open its doors to more non-traditional students]

[The call to increase enrolment is not always matched with the offer of increased resources]

[Any social provision that benefits the few has to be viewed as a luxury]

[Most of the economies of the UWI contributing territories have been experiencing negative growth]

Resource Constraints

In the discussion over the need to increase enrolment at UWI, the difficulty of providing the commensurate physical resources to match the greater numbers of students may be the greatest problem. With only a few exceptions, most of the economies of the UWI contributing territories have been experiencing negative growth and therefore have found it difficult to help fund their desire to see the university become more accessible.

UWI, the University of Guyana, the University of Technology (Jamaica) and the Northern Caribbean University (formerly the West Indies College, Jamaica) are unable to provide places for all those seeking a university education. Consequently, foreign universities and other deliverers of advanced training have taken advantage of the increased demand. New technologies, the globalization of services and greater cost effectiveness in education access have also influenced this trend. The regional demand has encouraged more aggressive marketing strategies and development thrusts from foreign higher education institutions.

UWI has never been able to offer places to all those who wish to read for a degree at the institution. Enrolment figures indicate that most faculties have already reached projected enrolment targets. Further, the reporting of overcrowding on the three campuses is now a factor included in most quality assurance reviews.

[Foreign universities and other deliverers of advanced training have taken advantage of the increased demand]

[The reporting of overcrowding on the three campuses is now a factor included in most quality assurance reviews]

Congested Spaces

There is strain on the facilities and undoubtedly this has a deleterious effect on the quality of provision. The problem is more obvious on the Mona campus, and many believe that Jamaica's broader economic problems have slowed the expansion of the facilities. Further, even within this context the students are being asked to contribute to the cost of their education (20 per cent of the economic cost, a policy determined by the University Council and supported by the regional governments).

Overcrowded lecture theatres and cramped tutorial rooms are a recipe for frustration. Commuting students who fight traffic and scramble for parking space in the evenings find the campus environment unfriendly. One academic described the situation as a "cocktail for stress". Perhaps unsurprisingly, efforts to strengthen alumni relations yield results only relatively slowly and many graduates are not easily swayed into giving back to UWI.

Mature Students

The return to higher education of larger numbers of mature students creates further challenges for UWI. These students, primarily professionals, are more discriminating. They are not easily satisfied with the quality of teaching and learning, especially that which they may experience in the part-time and distance education programmes. The demands of work and family add to their stress levels.

While the dilemmas are real, the challenge for UWI is finding the right ingredients to make the mix of increased enrolment and the provision of the resources to support, maintain and enhance the quality of the teaching/learning experience.

As noted earlier, one part of the solution must be the expansion of the provision within other tertiary level institutions where university-level courses are delivered. Consideration is also being given to the establishment of a more formally constructed Caribbean higher education system that would give certain community colleges associate status within a UWI network. The expansion of distance education will also alleviate the stress placed on campus facilities. The establishment of the virtual university through Web-based courses and greater use of distance modes of delivery are other options that can make UWI more accessible and affordable to more students.

[Students are being asked to contribute more to the cost of their education]

[The expansion of distance education will also alleviate the stress placed on campus facilities]

Language and Access

Caribbean linguists, educators and policy makers have long debated issues that relate to deciding who should have access to public education provision. Competence in the language of instruction has always appeared at the forefront of the discourse, both here and elsewhere. For example, some years ago a Chinese student called the Language Unit at the School of Continuing Studies at the University of Toronto requesting to take French. The administrative assistant expressed dismay at the request, since, in her words, "She can hardly speak English!" Her col-

[Is competence in English a requirement to study another language?]

league asked: "Since when is competence in English a requirement to study another language?"

Competence in English and UWI

Testing competence in the language of instruction at higher education institutions is common elsewhere. The Test of English as a Foreign Language (TOEFL), the Michigan examination (MELAB), and the CanTest or the International English Language Testing Systems (IELTS) are used extensively throughout North America and Great Britain, but the tests are administered to students whose first language is not English. (Further pressure for such testing is derived from the fact that academics in universities have also complained about the quality of writing of their English-speaking nationals.)

Similar issues have arisen at UWI. At its meeting in May 1996, the University Academic Committee agreed in principle to the proposal for the compulsory English Language Proficiency Test (ELPT) for all undergraduate applicants to UWI. The introduction of this test had widespread support, both within and outside the academic community. The proposal, emanating from the Mona campus, had the subsequent support of the Cave Hill campus. In February 1996, the Mona Campus Academic Board approved the proposal to test certain categories of degree applicants in English language proficiency. The board also decided that the test would be part of the selection mechanism for admission into UWI.

[Tests are administered to students whose first language is not English]

Testing Time

In 1998, for the first time, fifty-eight applicants were not accepted to UWI solely on the basis of failure in the ELPT. The Cave Hill and St Augustine campuses and the Faculty of Pure and Applied Sciences, Mona campus, all expressed strong reservations about the test's introduction and showed concern about the possible effects the test might have on the number of applications and offers made. The Cave Hill and St Augustine campuses accepted the test as a diagnostic tool but did not endorse its use in the admission and matriculation mechanisms; this appears to be a reasonable position.

[The test would be part of the selection mechanism for admission into UWI]

The test has also caused concern among applicants to UWI, particularly where a campus has excluded applicants who failed the test even though they fulfilled the stated normal and/or lower level matriculation requirements. It is true that faculties may select the "most qualified" applicants on the basis of grades obtained in CXC/GCE examinations. When an applicant is not offered a place, however, even when he or she has met the stated UWI requirements, it seems to many to represent an injustice.

[The Cave Hill and St Augustine campuses accepted the test as a diagnostic tool but did not endorse its use in the admissions and matriculation mechanisms]

[Faculties may select the "most qualified" applicants]

Assisting "Failures"

There is no denying that many undergraduates at UWI (in all disciplines across all faculties) demonstrate unacceptable English language skills in their academic work. Evidence from the Department of Language, Linguistics and Philosophy at Mona has suggested that the problem is much greater at that campus than at the Cave Hill and St Augustine campuses.

UWI offers Fundamentals of English (UC010) to its students as an opportunity to correct English language deficiencies. At Mona the large number of students required to take UC010 puts tremendous strain on the resources of the Department of Language, Linguistics and Philosophy. UWI must decide whether it wishes to continue to offer remedial programmes to less proficient students, who might otherwise never have the opportunity to benefit from higher education. If it does so, however, it must commit the necessary resources for effective delivery of a developmental programme.

Language Barrier

[Many undergraduates demonstrate poor English language skills]

One view that has been expressed at meetings of the Mona Board of the Faculty of Arts and Education (previously the Faculty of Arts and General Studies) and the Mona Academic Board is that UC010 should be phased out and applicants with an unsatisfactory level of English language proficiency should be refused entry into UWI.

It is unlikely that the entry situation at Mona will change soon, even though recent results of CXC–CSEC examinations have shown that there has been some improvement in the performance of Jamaican students in English; that is, there has been an increase in the number of students obtaining Grades I or II. Prospective students from the Eastern Caribbean are already indicating that Mona is not the campus of choice because of its policy on English. The policy also means that a Jamaican student who applies to the Cave Hill or St Augustine campuses will not meet the same fate as his or her counterpart at Mona if he or she fails the ELPT.

[Applicants with an unsatisfactory level of English language proficiency should be refused entry into UWI]

Language and Equity

The poor English language skills being demonstrated by significant numbers of undergraduates and the lack of adequate resources to offer remedial programmes have been noted. There are also broader social factors that should be considered. One proposition is that the limits placed on UWI cannot allow it to offer developmental courses to students who "failed" to reach the standard required for success at university-level courses. Reality, however, should make us to rethink that position. There are too many social and economic indices for Jamaica that tell us that UWI does not have the luxury to be severely discriminatory in its entry practices if it wishes to make adequate contribution to regional development.

Teachers of English believe, with some degree of validity, that students at all levels of the education system in the region are affected by their competency in English. We must, however, be cautious in making the inferential leap from correlations between failure in English and failure in other subjects. Correlation is not causation. Even if there is positive correlation between the two variables, too little is known about the intervening variables that might affect outcomes.

'English Standards'

The CXC–CSEC examinations test skills and competencies developed by the students' academic experience, primarily at the completion of Grade 11. UWI is fairly confident when it says that success at CXC is a reliable indicator of success at the university. Enough is known of educational psychology to accept that motivation, economic and social circumstances, and other factors also contribute to success. UWI should offer its weaker students opportunities to correct deficiencies – it cannot do that by denying those students a place because their English is "not

[CXC is a reliable indicator of success at the university]

redeemable". UWI's efforts to widen access could be harmed if the results of the ELPT affect numbers applications or admissions.

Linguists and teachers of English accept the soundness of the argument that language acquisition is developmental and students' rhetorical skills shift according to genre, situation and time. On the one hand, linguists extol the richness and vibrancy of creole and demand that it takes it pride of place, yet, on the other hand they lament the poor English skills that students demonstrate. The majority of West Indians are born hearing the dialects in our stories and our songs. They interface with it in our literature. Let the university provide the resources to increase students' capacity to read and write in another language (English, if necessary) at levels that reflect university standards.

Language Democracy

[Language acquisition is developmental and students' rhetorical skills shift according to genre, situation and time]

The university should not create barriers. If we say that West Indians should be multilingual then it should be accepted throughout the education system.

There are those who posit the view that the aggressive use of English in a region of multiple languages and dialects has an underdeveloping effect on the people of the region. However, the significance of the use of English in regional and international academia, business, and industry must be emphasized. Weakness in the language use of the learner should not, in itself, be a barrier to higher education.

[Let the university provide the resources to increase students' capacity to read and write in another language]

Migration and Development

In many countries, both developing and developed, significant numbers of students study abroad. The World Bank has recognized that the benefits from this practice can be substantiated as students are exposed to ideas, techniques and entire fields of study that differ from what is offered at home. Not only the students but the countries as a whole can benefit from such study (World Bank 2000).

In the case of the Caribbean, however, study is often the student's first step to resettling abroad. About one third of foreign students studying in the United States do not return to their home countries. While there is information on how many leave the English-speaking Caribbean for colleges and universities in the United States, Canada and the United Kingdom, how many receive government scholarships and the overall costs of these scholarships, it is not easy to determine how many return to the region upon completion of their studies.

✢ *Where Do They Go?*

Every year hundreds of students receive academic scholarships in the United States. In one year alone, two hundred Jamaicans received academic scholarships tenable at US colleges and universities. A few also go to Canada, mainly to Ontario, and a smaller number venture to the United Kingdom. Overall, it is difficult to determine the number of students from the English-speaking Caribbean who take this route to higher education.

Although studying outside the region is not as novel these days as it was in the past, a degree from a foreign university can still be impressive, whether or not anyone bothers to check the reputation of the university. To the less discriminating consumer, that the product is imported is the more important factor. With full scholarships being offered, students who think they meet the academic requirements go after these scholarships.

The reality is that the cost of overseas instruction, even to students who are on "full academic scholarships", is considerable. Further, even if the student's family is paying directly for the overseas education, there is the potential negative consequence for the sending country. Because relatively few students return, the sending country does not usually benefit directly. The region must make every effort to keep its able young people.

Funding Open Access: Carrots for Quality Candidates

It is believed that many of the more academically successful graduates of Caribbean secondary schools do not enter UWI. Instead, they are sought after and recruited by foreign colleges and universities. There is evidence that recruiters in Barbados, Jamaica, and Trinidad and Tobago find places and secure scholarships for graduates of regional secondary schools in several prestigious higher education institutions in Canada and the United States.

[It is not easy to determine how many return to the region upon completion of their studies]

[In one year alone, two hundred Jamaicans received academic scholarships tenable at US colleges and universities]

[Students who think they meet the academic requirements go after these scholarships]

[Weakness in the language use of the learner should not, in itself, be a barrier to higher education]

Recruitment and admissions officers send teams to the region each year to lure our secondary school students. Students who attend these "fairs" come away with brochures on admissions, housing and employment possibilities, convinced that higher education opportunities overseas are more lucrative and easier to access.

[The cost of overseas instruction, even to students who are on "full academic scholarships", is considerable]

✥ External Funding

The *Jamaican Observer* (8 June 1999) reported that Jamaican teenagers obtained US$13 million in scholarships to some of the best colleges and universities in the United States. Aid packages varied from US$19,000 per year to US$34,000 per year for a four-year period. Many Trinidadian students received similarly attractive scholarships, some valued up to US$80,000. These scholarships do not include athletic scholarships, which gifted Caribbean athletes, especially from Jamaica, have come to rely upon.

[Recruiters in Barbados, Jamaica, and Trinidad and Tobago find places and secure scholarships for graduates of regional secondary schools in several prestigious higher education institutions in Canada and the United States]

Family connections appear to contribute to the migration of some of the region's youth. Also, while the cost of higher education might be less expensive in the region, the availability of scholarships and bursaries in the United States to international students makes studying overseas an attractive option. Recent statistics show that approximately two thousand students from the English-speaking Caribbean are enrolled in US colleges and universities. Initiatives that would give the best students the opportunity to enter UWI would also help to fulfil longer term strategic objectives.

At a conference of the Northeast Region of Caribbean Students held at the Massachusetts Institute of Technology in Boston in April 1999, students from the English-speaking Caribbean indicated that apart from the wide choice of programmes of study, they chose to study in the United States primarily because of the financial assistance offered to them. When financial assistance did not fully cover tuition and living costs, the students said that they could work and study. By contrast, this option is not a convenient arrangement in the Caribbean region nor is part-time work available to the extent that could adequately augment students' income.

[The availability of scholarships and bursaries in the United States to international students makes studying overseas an attractive option]

✥ University Scholarships

At UWI a total of 179 scholarship funds and bursaries are available on an annual basis. From these, 549 awards are made. Included in these are the prestigious regional University Open Scholarships, which are available to students across the three campuses, and the ten Cable and Wireless Sir Frank Worrell Scholarships. UWI currently awards ten Open Scholarships each year, for which approximately two thousand secondary school students apply. Fifteen Government Exhibitions are also awarded annually. In the case of the UWI Open Scholarships, the award covers the full cost of tuition and maintenance for the duration of study. The Sir Frank Worrell Scholarships are valued at US$5,000. The number of scholarships has, however, remained unchanged over many years, during which time UWI has expanded greatly. There should be a significant increase in the number of scholarships awarded.

Other scholarships and bursaries are administered by UWI on behalf of donors. These awards are primarily made on academic merit. However, there are also bursaries offered to students where financial need is the main criterion for the award.

More Prize Money

Faculty and department prizes are also awarded across the campuses for outstanding performance of students. The value of these prizes is considerably lower, however. Finally, on each campus full-time students experiencing financial difficulties may apply for loans or grants ranging from US$400 to US$1,000. On the St Augustine campus the loan is only available to final-year students.

Overall, the value of undergraduate scholarships range between US$650 and US$5,000, excepting the University Scholarships. On the other hand, tuition fees for students from contributing countries range from approximately US$2,000 to US$7,500, depending on the campus and faculty. The point is that in relation to costs of an undergraduate programme, the value of other scholarships and bursaries fall well below what would be required to fully assist students.

Implications for UWI

UWI is not able to offer all eligible candidates scholarships and/or financial assistance that could match the offers of US colleges and universities. It is, however, important that UWI recognizes that any investment in the future of the people of the region, no matter how small, is a

[They chose to study in the United States primarily because of the financial assistance offered to them]

[The number of scholarships has, however, remained unchanged over many years, during which time UWI has expanded greatly]

[An expansion of financial incentives through scholarships and awards to the most deserving must be included]

tangible contribution to the expansion of educational opportunities and talent development through higher education. As UWI addresses strategies related to widening and deepening access, an expansion of financial incentives through scholarships and awards to the most deserving must be included if it intends to remain competitive in an arena filled with other deliverers of higher education programmes.

The Offices of Admissions on all campuses should incorporate into their programmes for the secondary schools scholarship information that would encourage eligible candidates to choose UWI. This should point to the commitment of UWI to provide funding for outstanding applicants. Any initiative that would give the best students the opportunity to enter UWI would be helpful in fulfilling strategic objectives in the long term. In the short term, for example, it could also strengthen recruitment into the Mona Faculty of Pure and Applied Sciences, which is experiencing difficulty in attracting sufficient undergraduates.

Marketing Approach

Beyond vigorous marketing and recruitment drives, summer science enhancement/enrichment programmes, open house and research days, scholarships that target outstanding science students based on CXC examinations results could greatly encourage prospective undergraduates to choose UWI over overseas institutions. This latter has recently been established. Every year thousands of Grade 11 students in the region sit CSEC examinations and each year now CXC makes awards to nine students who perform exceptionally well in these examinations. The recipients of these awards receive publicity along with a substantial monetary award to assist them in meeting tuition and maintenance costs at UWI.

The Quality Assurance System of UWI

It should be noted that before any quality assurance system is implemented it is essential that an appropriate financial balance be established between the demands imposed by quality assurance and the results expected from the system. In general, there is a need for clarity of the purposes of quality assurance (including the potential benefits to stakeholders and the institution). Without this there is a danger that the system produces defensive and negative reactions in academic and other staff and few gains. Clarity can produce greater openness and a more positive approach to improving quality.

[It is essential that an appropriate financial balance be established between the demands imposed by quality assurance and the results expected]

Undergraduate Provision at UWI

The Board for Undergraduate Studies has responsibility for general policy at undergraduate level, quality assurance and quality audit and the preservation of regionality. The Office of Board for Undergraduate Studies carries out the policies and directives of the Board for Undergraduate Studies, with the Quality Assurance Unit within the Office of the Board for Undergraduate Studies, with staff on each campus having specific responsibility for developing and implementing the system of quality assurance and quality audit.

The work of the Quality Assurance Unit includes:

- organizing quality assurance reviews of undergraduate and postgraduate taught programmes, supporting the major self-
- assessment that is undertaken before each review, and guiding the work of review teams during the visits and drafting the reports of the reviews;
- conducting audits of the learning environment, such as those into the operation of the Summer School, registration procedures, foundation courses, the operation of the libraries and so on;

- participating in activities and visits to monitor quality assurance within the development of articulation agreements between UWI and regional tertiary level institutions; and
- supporting professional faculties and departments in preparations for accreditation visits, with a particular focus on the quality assurance procedures being employed (and with, when necessary and useful, a quality audit – that is, a review of these quality assurance procedures).

UWI Quality Assurance Review Process

At UWI periodic reviews of the teaching of all the different disciplines are undertaken in a five-year cycle. These reviews are quite separate from the academic assessment of members of staff, which is the responsibility of the Campus or University Appointments Committee. Quality assurance reviews do not assess individuals and, in contrast to the assessment of staff members for promotion or contract renewal, the internal quality assurance system at UWI is of a formative and developmental nature.

The intent is to assure stakeholders of the continued high quality and standards of UWI's academic work and to enhance that work.

[The intent is to assure stakeholders of the continued high quality and standards of UWI's academic work and to enhance that work]

Effects of Meetings

When a particular discipline has been selected for review, a member of the Quality Assurance Unit meets with the academic staff who teach the discipline. This meeting is intended to orient the academic staff to the purposes and procedures of the review; to allow for questions about the process; to ensure that the members of staff are clear as to the purpose and nature of the self-assessment; and to provide for discussion on any discipline-specific issues.

A review team, usually of three or four members, is appointed with representation from the same subject on another campus and two or three independent members. The independent members are one or two senior academics from outside the Caribbean region and a person with professional expertise in the discipline, from the region but external to UWI.

The Self-Assessment

In the months prior to the visit of the Quality Assurance Review Team academic staff undertake a self-assessment. This has the goal of examining the stated aims and objectives of the teaching of the discipline and determining the extent to which they are being realized. The process also identifies issues that are having an impact on the learning experience of the students. While there is much descriptive material in a self-assessment report, the primary aim of the self-assessment is to understand, analyse and evaluate, not merely to describe or defend. The self-assessment report should result from wide-ranging discussions among colleagues; take account of information available from students; graduates and employers; and be generally agreed on by the colleagues concerned.

The report of the self-assessment begins with a statement of the aims and objectives of the teaching of the discipline and how these relate to the mission statement and/or the strategic plan of UWI, the campus and the department. The aims and objectives of the teaching of the discipline are of central importance as they set the context in which the quality of education provided is evaluated. The review team uses these statements as a guide and investigates the extent to which the aims and objectives are being realized.

[The primary aim of the self-assessment is to understand, analyse and evaluate, not merely to describe or defend]

Practical Objectives

Aims indicate what the department is trying to achieve in terms of the provision for the students, including the curriculum, teaching, learning and assessment methods, resources, and quality assurance procedures. The learning objectives refer to the outcomes desired and are linked to standards. The objectives should be specific, appropriate and practical, not simply aspirations that cannot realistically be achieved by the students.

The remainder of the self-assessment report demonstrates how the aims and objectives are being met by the teaching of the discipline. The material is considered under five headings: Curriculum; Teaching and Learning; Student Profile, Assessment and Learning Outcomes; Resources for Teaching and Learning; and Quality Assurance and Enhancement. Issues to be addressed in each section are indicated in a handbook developed by the Quality Assurance Unit. Not all issues are relevant to all disciplines, and in some cases staff may wish to include others. The final section contains a summary and recommendations for developing the discipline.

Evidence is provided to support statements made in the report and it is this evidence that forms the foundation for all conclusions. (An indicative list of the evidence needed for a review is given in appendix 2.) The review team looks for the links between the claims and the evidence and, after the visit to the campus, for consistency among the evidence from different sources. The final report, with appropriate supporting information, is sent to the members of the review team, who use it to help identify areas that might be usefully investigated further during the visit of the team.

Reviewing the Self-Review

The review team reviews the self-assessment report and its appendices and makes a four- to five-day visit to the campus. This visit has the purpose of testing the validity of the self-assessment report. While on campus the review team examines other data and documentation, and it also has meetings with academic and technical staff, with undergraduate and postgraduate students, with graduates of the programmes and employers of graduates, and with senior faculty and management personnel of the campus. The team inspects related teaching facilities, visits laboratories and the library, and observes teaching sessions.

The review team prepares and submits its written report, which is distributed by the Quality Assurance Unit. As a result of the self-assessment and the visit and report of the review team, the academic staff identifies issues for further consideration. The head of department reports on action taken following the review to Faculty Board, which reports to the campus Academic Board. The campus principal has overall responsibility for monitoring the follow-up process. A year after the review, the department reports to the Board for Undergraduate Studies and the Board for Graduate Studies and Research, through the Academic Board, outlining the activities that have occurred.

Evaluation of Research and Publication Activity

[Output is judged against international standards in research, scholarship and publication]

The UWI Office of Research (which works within the Board for Graduate Studies and Research) conducts evaluations of the research and publication activity of departments, centres and institutes. The intention is to assess the quality and quantity of research and publication activity, to encourage its growth, and to guide strategic planning and policy. The evaluation is undertaken at the same time as a quality assurance review. In a research evaluation the output is judged against international standards in research, scholarship and publication.

Central to a research evaluation is an assessment of the published works in the unit during the assessment period. UWI has adopted a broad definition of research and publication output, with any form of output embodying the outcomes of scholarship, research or professional work being eligible.

Thus, in addition to academic and professional publications, conference papers and technical reports, output can include new materials and products, whether in patent or otherwise, artistic performances, exhibitions or events, and work published in non-print media. Other aspects of a unit's work to be taken into account include the numbers of research students and advanced degrees awarded during the assessment period, the level of research funding, and other external indicators.

External Scrutiny

An external academic member of the quality assurance review team considers the quality and quantity of the research and publication using the documentation provided. Quantitative data on research activity is considered in relation to the number of academic staff, in order to avoid bias against small units and heavy teaching loads. The reports include commentary on the activity level of the unit along with judgements as to the quantity and quality of the research, publications and other work.

[Reviewers assess the quality of the output]

Reviewers assess the quality of the output on the basis of the quality and standards of the publication medium, attaching greater weight to work published under a well-established rigorous editorial and refereeing standard. Other activities are understood to have similar standards if, for example, a publication compares well with work published by a leading journal or is presented at a conference of recognized international standing.

Generally, items involving peer judgement rate higher than other items. The reviewer takes account of indicators of peer esteem, such as external research funding, and evidence that identifies members of staff as international leaders in their field. Current and future plans and the methods for promoting, managing and monitoring research are considered. The reviewer identifies evidence of the vitality of the research culture and judges the potential impact of the unit's research programme upon future research directions and within applications of the research.

Enhancing the Quality and Standards of Postgraduate Degrees

At UWI the Board for Graduate Studies and Research has the responsibility for monitoring and enhancing the quality and standards of postgraduate and research degrees. Universities need to evaluate the extent to which they ensure appropriate standards in the research degrees awarded and that adequate training and support are provided to enable students to attain those standards.

Issues to be taken into account in such an evaluation include the approval of projects, skills training, supervision, feedback, assessment and appeals. An evaluation should consider the working of the procedures that seek to ensure that research projects undertaken are suitable for the programmes of study and that the students possess the skills, knowledge and aptitudes required for successful completion of the project. The resources needed to support the projects – including staff, facilities and materials – must be available throughout the projects and student progress must be adequately supported and monitored.

Research Students

Many research students need training to gain the skills needed to design and complete their programmes effectively. An evaluation should consider whether, prior to entry or during the programmes, there is the development of these skills. Students should receive sufficient support and direction to enable them to succeed in their studies, and an evaluation should consider this. It should also consider the arrangements for feedback to students.

An evaluation should determine the adequacy of the mechanisms that enable feedback to be provided to the university by research students and their supervisors. Research degree assessment processes should operate rigorously, consistently and fairly and be communicated clearly to students and supervisors. The evaluation should assess the provision in this regard. Finally, independent, formal, fair, open and efficient procedures should be available to deal with complaints from research students about the university's provision and decisions.

Governance and Management

Governing bodies of higher education institutions have historically not been designed for strategic management but rather as representative bodies of a wide constituency of interests. For example, UWI Statutes outline the composition of each Campus Council, the campus governing body. Apart from the senior management leadership there is representation of the regional governments, non-governmental organizations, other tertiary level institutions, graduates and students, and non-academic staff.

It has been suggested that, in practice, a substantial proportion of the members of an institution's governing body may make only a small contribution to the work of the body, often due to insufficient knowledge. A small group within the governing body tends to control the overall process of governance and policy development. The process of selection is often strongly influenced by existing member's informal networks, in particular, those of the chair, who often has a key role in recruiting other members.

The members of the governing body who have informal access to information are in a stronger position to understand the issues and make contributions. This effect can be heightened by the type and quantity of information formally provided to the governing body by the senior management team. It has been noted that two distinct models of decision making in tertiary educational institutions may be identified: the professional and the managerial models. In the former model, the academic hierarchy makes the major strategic decisions, while in the latter the governing body and senior management team lead the implementation of centrally driven policies and objectives.

[An evaluation should determine the adequacy of mechanisms that enable feedback to be provided to the university]

[Open and efficient procedures should be available to deal with complaints from research students]

[A small group within the governing body tends to control the overall process of governance and policy development]

[In recent years there have been shifts from the professional towards the managerial model in many tertiary institutions]

A Shift in Approach

In recent years there have been shifts from the professional towards the managerial model in many tertiary institutions, although some institutions may be straddling the two models. There is now increased emphasis on concepts such as efficiency, meeting the needs of the market and entrepreneurialism. The changes have also given governing bodies a clear monitoring role. Governing bodies are expected to bring together planning, resource allocation and accountability and to link the academic, physical and financial aspects. It is the role of the governing body to develop a strategic vision and associated plans so that the institution maintains its academic vitality and financial viability and meets societal needs. The strategic survival of the institution is the responsibility of the governing body, which has the responsibility for ensuring that the senior management team of the institution identifies the priorities effectively.

Strategic Planning

[The strategic survival of the institution is the responsibility of the governing body]

The vice chancellor or president of a university is now often seen as both the academic leader and chief executive of the institution, although any individual will possess his or her own particular emphases. The chief executive has the responsibility for undertaking strategic analysis and developing the strategic plans, to be approved by the governing body, that will deliver the governing body's strategic vision. The chief executive also has responsibility for delivery of operational plans, managing his or her executive colleagues, and accounting to the governing body as to the effectiveness with which he or she is discharging the governing body's business, particularly the implementation of the operational plans.

[The chief executive has the responsibility for undertaking strategic analysis]

The chair of the governing body is particularly important in this structure and he or she must ensure that the members of senior management understand the body's strategic role and address strategic issues. The chair also ensures that the chief executive undertakes his responsibilities to the governing body and does not simply regard the governing body as a rubber-stamping formality. Some chairs may not provide adequate leadership if they are too closely guided by the chief executive.

[Some chairs may not provide adequate leadership if they are too closely guided by the chief executive]

Governing Body

The monitoring of the financial affairs of an institution is clearly an important role of its governing body and senior management. Most institutions have thorough systems for financial management, and the use of independent financial auditors provides further confidence in this aspect of the performance of the governing body and senior management.

There are, however, now often also explicit demands that a governing body and senior management team take a greater role regarding issues within academic development and academic quality assurance, although this does not yet appear to be the case in the Caribbean. At UWI, while there is now an integrated academic quality assurance system, the several governing bodies (Campus Councils, University Council) have so far taken a relatively limited direct role.

[At UWI, while there is now an academic quality assurance system, the several governing bodies have so far taken a relatively limited direct role]

✥ Knowing the Needs

A governing body has responsibility of identifying avenues for its direct contribution to the enhancement of the quality of academic provision. It should be involved in determining the institution's academic strategic plan, drawing on its knowledge of societal needs; in preparing procedures for monitoring the achievement of strategic objectives including the use of performance targets; and in the overall monitoring of the institution's strategic direction.

Senior management should monitor the institution's academic performance and students' achievement, and they should engage in an institution-wide approach to improving this achievement. Further, structures should be established to allow the academic staff to focus on teaching, scholarship and research, in order to ensure the continued currency of the work. Overall, the governing body must provide supportive and open governance while observing the boundaries between governance and management.

[Structures should be established to allow the academic staff to focus on teaching, scholarship and research]

Monitoring Outputs

The governing body should also monitor the performance of the senior management team, including the appraisal of the chief executive. It does not seem appropriate, however, for a governing body to have an obligation to monitor others' work but not be formally accountable for its own. Thus the efforts and accomplishments of a governing body in its various activities should be formally evaluated.

There should be public evidence presented so that members of the governing body can review and assess the performance of the body itself, and the governing body should be involved in quality assurance processes, including engaging in processes of self-assessment and analysis. It has been argued that if the governing body of an institution of higher or further education accepts its obligations for public accountability it will be better placed to argue for the autonomy, both academic and otherwise, that has been traditionally granted to such institutions.

[There should be public evidence presented so that members of the governing body can review and assess the performance of the body itself]

Public Confidence

The evaluations suggested above of the work of the governing body would have the intent of raising the quality of the work. This is not to say that individual appraisals should not be carried but, given the complex nature of interpersonal interactions within a group such as a governing body, it is the completed work and contribution of the body that is of most significance to the institution, rather than an analysis of the contributions of individuals. Further, given the demands on members of the governing body and in the expectation that its performance will be assessed, there is a need for:

- a public process for the appointment of members of the governing body;
- the appointment of well-informed members with adequate experience, skills and commitment rather than members only from a requirement of wide representation; and
- training and orientation for new members of a governing body.

[Consultation and competition should be applied while securing resources and services]

Senior Management

[Financial decisions should support the academic priorities]

The senior management team is responsible for ensuring that the institution follows responsible financial management methods. Appropriate principles of comparison, consultation and competition should be applied while securing resources and services. As these decisions will be

> [Strategic objectives need to be fully explained to and accepted by all members of staff]

externally audited they are not further discussed here. However, as management activity in higher education institutions should reflect the centrality of teaching and learning, financial decisions should support the academic priorities that have been identified.

Universities must have one focus of raising achievement and supporting the work of all learners. To this end, senior management should establish clear educational priorities and adopt appropriate measures of the quality and standards of the education delivered. The strategic objectives need to be fully explained to and accepted by all members of staff, with retention, achievement and progression targets being set. Performance should be monitored and evaluated and steps taken to secure improvement through self-assessment and other quality assurance procedures.

Quality assurance arrangements must be systematic and lead to priorities and targets for improvement being identified. Management should ensure that members of staff are involved in the institution's quality assurance arrangements. Personal leadership, rather than just management, is crucial here.

Globalization
Internal Quality and External Competition

Contradictory Trends

From the perspective of societies with histories and contemporary realities such as those that identify the Caribbean, globalization is best understood as a contradictory process. On the one hand, it speaks to a new and growing culture of openness and instant universal access – the much-desired level playing field. But at the same time, it consolidates and deepens traditional cleavages between rich and poor nations and sets them apart as uneven beneficiaries of the knowledge revolution that constitutes its primary driving force.

The fact remains, furthermore, despite the seductive rhetoric of the dawn of borderlessness, that the basic organizing principle of globalization is the nation state. In effect, this means that the global contest for resources, respected sovereignty, and even survival, is played out as a conflict between rich and poor nations and strong and weak nationalisms. In this re-engineered arena, the critical resource is organized knowledge, which feeds the new information and communications technologies that are distinguishing features of the new dispensation. The problem from the perspective of the marginalized is that the global two-way flow is unequal, with widely different territorial outcomes.

[Globalization is best understood as a contradictory process]

[The basic organizing principle of globalization is the nation state]

[In this re-engineered arena, the critical resource is organized knowledge]

Higher Education as a Global Industry

A principal effect of these deeply transforming circumstances is that higher education, the arena of new knowledge development, is emerging as a global mega-industry. The phenomenal rate at which education is being industrialized, pivots UWI in new ways, redefines its mandate and calls upon it to perform multiple roles emanating from the contradictory features of the process.

In the Caribbean, where these developments can be viewed up front and first hand, institutions of higher education, such as UWI, are immersed in a way that may suggest the tightening grip around the throat by strange hands. As a perception, which may be real or imagined, the critical issue is the strategic response that will determine not only survival but effective adaptation, transformation and emergence as a more viable force.

In addition, dozens of these institutions advancing the global industrialization of the Caribbean higher education sector – a process enabled by the new information and communications technologies as well as the new trade liberalization ideology – are now enrolling Caribbean students at home in large numbers.

Open Terrain

[The migration of non-national universities into the region is both physical and virtual]

The migration of non-national universities into the region is both physical and virtual. With respect to the former, they are finding market niches, meeting demand and establishing positive relations with host countries. In terms of the latter, there is an expectation that they will provide significant leadership in producing the first generation of cyber-students and otherwise facilitating the growth of the global culture of student-centred "quality" education.

While the initial reaction of some national institutions was marked by caution and concern, the warmth with which non-national institutions have been received by many governments and private sectors has created the basis for rethinking the future nature of the tertiary sector and its vital role in human resource development. More often than not the arrival of these institutions is surrounded by insufficient public knowledge, which means that it is no easy task to convert local suspicion into practical international cooperation.

UWI's Response

[UWI has adopted a strategic response that augurs well for the region]

UWI has adopted a strategic response that augurs well for the region, including, of course, itself as the premier regional institution of higher learning. In the first instance it has facilitated the establishment and growth of a network of regional tertiary level institutions (ACTI) in order to effectively plan with one vision for the regions' educational needs. Second, it has directly engaged and also assisted some tertiary level institutions in forging mutual cooperative arrangements with non-national institutions that are internationally accredited. Third, it has launched a quality assurance agenda which will serve to ensure that what is offered to Caribbean citizens is subject to scientific scrutiny.

The posture, then, is that the presence of multiple carriers of higher education will be a long-term feature of the region and that "planned diversity" is the way to go with respect to radically advancing the pace of human resource development. This proactive approach is based upon UWI's recognition of its own competitive strengths as well as its awareness of the need to be flexible and innovative, with respect to changing circumstances, in seeking to serve the interests of its stakeholders.

Effective Leadership

Success in this approach will require effective leadership, particularly as it is now fully accepted that with current and projected funding, UWI, the University of Technology (Jamaica), the Northern Caribbean University and the University of Guyana will be challenged to meet the rapidly growing demand for higher education. Cooperation across the sector can result in rational planning and efficiency gains but only if there is transparency and an understanding that publicly approved notions of the regional interest should be the guiding principle.

In this open market reality, regional institutions will have to be bold and innovative, strategic and committed. They can only do so by continuing to show their relevance and demonstrating high quality. Those who believe that regional institutions are at risk may be concerned about these institutions' ability and resolve to rise to the challenge. The evidence indicates that UWI is rising to a sense of its own maturity. This is demonstrated in the steady manner and perceptive leadership style with which it is negotiating the seemingly contradictory forces of planned diversity.

✣ *Internationalization*

The words "internationalization" and "globalization" have assumed distinct historical meanings and therefore discernible "politics" in development discourse. For this reason, they ought not to be used interchangeably as they are invested with very different explanatory powers. By using them within the context of structural transformations in the Caribbean higher education sector (or any other marginalized space, for that matter) it is possible to identify these different ideological and economic processes.

Internationalization is the process whereby societies are seen to be in a state of constant intercultural exchange and cooperation. Its historic nature is defined by human migration that flows in multiple directions, leading to the creation of new cultural experiences and forms of creolization. As a process, it is driven primarily at the level of the individual who has no overt or formal political objective. It recognizes no hierarchy of centres and therefore proceeds with a benign mutualism.

⁜ Globalization

Globalization, however, is altogether a very different process: it is a highly organized, politically shaped economic agenda and is conceived and determined by powerful entities such as expansionist states and transnational corporations. These agencies have as objectives the control and redesign of targeted spaces for the explicit purpose of achieving market influence, maximizing self-interest and establishing structures of power.

Furthermore, globalization is defined primarily by its ideology of cultural penetration and economic domination and in the past five hundred years has been a project of the North Atlantic industrializing world. Within its political tradition are relations of power such as colonialism and cultural hegemony. Its present shape and immediate future are centred in the knowledge revolution. As such, it has mobilized new information and communications technologies, as well as educational pedagogies, in order to more sharply define its desired international division of possibilities.

Critical Distinction

While it is possible to identify overlaps in the functions of both processes, or even stages of growth that may suggest an evolution from one to another, internationalization and globalization are sufficiently discernible to enable meaningful analysis with respect to levels of activity within a given locality – in this instance the Caribbean tertiary education sector. As one of many sites in the developing world that is targeted by North Atlantic educational entrepreneurs the Caribbean tertiary sector is an excellent arena within which to assess and understand the tensions and contests between national development needs and globalizing, non-national agendas.

Traditional Educational Strategies

Since its encounter with modernity, the Caribbean has sought to identify its strategic interests in terms of pursuing the creative expansion of an education system for human resource development and management by engaging both processes of internationalism and globalization. As such, the evolution of a political economy of education in the region featured an ad hoc search for special concessionary opportunities, niche finding in some cases, which enabled it to meet some basic needs.

In earlier times the predicament internal to this circumstance was posed in terms of how best to connect internationally the region's institutions in order to benefit from educational networks and systems. Invariably the focus was on student migration and academic cooperation for scholars. Today, the question is posed differently, and it suggests the existence of an ambivalent politics: how to exploit the opportunities and challenges offered by globalization (while making a meaningful international contribution) but protect past gains and present achievements from its subversive and corrosive capabilities. Globalization, the post-Seattle world now accepts, is very much a double-edged sword.

The 1992 World Bank Report

In 1992 the Population and Human Resource Division of the World Bank conducted a major study of the Caribbean tertiary education sector. The overwhelming significance of its findings was that there existed a crisis of access, which meant that a chronic human resource shortage was inhibiting sustainable development. The anatomy of the crisis of access was explained in terms of the failure of traditional models of delivering mass higher education, particularly the insufficiency of internationalization as a strategy for widening and expanding enrolment at levels consistent with the needs of the new democratic dispensation.

The World Bank projected that nothing short of a revolution in access to the tertiary sector is a prerequisite for sustainable development within the region. Using data for 1988 to 1990 it showed that the

[The Caribbean tertiary sector is an excellent arena within which to assess and understand the tensions and contests between national development needs and globalizing, non-national agendas]

[Globalization, the post-Seattle world now accepts, is very much a double-edged sword]

[The World Bank projected that nothing short of a revolution in access to the tertiary sector is a prerequisite for sustainable development within the region]

anglophone region was located at the bottom of the hemispheric ladder with respect to enrolment of the relevant age cohort. Less than 5 per cent were enrolled and had benefited from access. In the hemisphere the average was close to 20 per cent – driven at the top by North America, which had moved beyond 40 per cent, but characterized by rapid catch-up policies in Latin America and the Spanish-speaking Caribbean subregion.

Inadequate Approaches

But UWI itself has long been a driving force and a major beneficiary of the internationalized education sector, which featured the global mobilization of supportive friends of the region. What the World Bank called into question was the limitation of the transforming role of these arrangements. The following expressions of the UWI-led internationalization of the sector were identified:

- the promotion of student access to "foreign" universities and other academic and training programmes through the traditional correspondence modality;
- the facilitation of the use of national and foreign scholarships to finance student travel and study in foreign universities, mostly in the United Kingdom;
- the encouragement of the use of private funds to access United Kingdom, United States and Canadian institutions;
- the encouragement of access to Caribbean universities and other institutions by non-nationals, who were invited through study abroad schemes to engage Caribbean programmes; and
- the creation of collaborative arrangements between Caribbean-based institutions and foreign-based institutions with respect to jointly delivered and jointly owned programmes.

Limits of Elitism

The insufficiency of internationalization was illustrated with respect to its limited impact, as well as its tendency to reinforce elitist concepts and methods of access even among the limited number within the privileged social classes. The notion of the foreign-trained scholar, the "returning" academic, was established and elevated within the iconography of higher education.

In effect, those who travelled "out" were seen as miles ahead and a cut above those who stayed "in", particularly those who accessed foreign universities by correspondence – that was seen as a kind of low-technology distance mode, developed to facilitate colonials. UWI, however, acquired considerable prestige within this world. In the process it validated internationalization as an effective way to promote collaborative relations for mutual development.

While internationalism was perceived as a positive process, particularly among its minority beneficiaries, the World Bank report showed it as a strategy of elite reproduction. It did so by associating its use with the reproduction of constraining attitudes that have hampered local institutional growth.

Furthermore, it is seen as having done little to reduce significantly the cost of higher education for the student and the state. As a result, the expansion of the regional tertiary sector became heavily reliant upon bilateral and multilateral agencies, the World Bank, as well as United Nations agencies.

Open Policy

Beginning with the leadership of Vice Chancellor Alistair McIntyre, UWI was crucial in finding a strategic response to the crisis of access by mobilizing all stakeholders to take collective responsibility for a sharp turnaround. A critical element of this strategy was to expand radically traditional patterns of internationalization by setting up special machinery within UWI to expose students to opportunities for study in foreign universities, and to open the region's doors to foreign students within a network of exchanges and cooperative agreements.

A second element of the strategy was the development of ACTI, a significant step in the building of local capacity that also deepened international access arrangements. ACTI has had considerable success in alleviating the crisis outlined by the World Bank.

"Offshore" Universities

Meanwhile, however, the paradigm of higher education access was shifting rapidly. The balance of change tilted in the direction of globalization as opposed to internationalism. Globalization within the tertiary sector manifested itself in three principal ways. First, the region experienced a proliferation of foreign universities, mostly registered as "offshore" institutions that are transacting business within most communities. At least one of these universities, the St George's Medical School in Grenada, has received a national charter. It has been described as an "offshore school that has come on shore" – and is already seen to be behaving in a way that suggests its status as a "resident alien".

The critical development on this score is that dozens of foreign universities have arrived in the Caribbean to do business with students in their homes. The economics directing this product intervention has had a significant impact upon the Caribbean tertiary sector, even though most of these universities cater at best minimally for nationals of the countries in which they reside. As offshore universities, they are scattered throughout the archipelago like the castles of expansionist kingdoms, and most are welcomed with open arms by their hosts, the traditional stakeholders of UWI.

Shopping for Education

Second, and this is an example of internationalism evolving into globalization, US universities especially have actively recruited and are importing thousands of young Caribbean nationals for enrolment in their programmes. They do this in collaboration with Caribbean educators who identify and sign up high school prospects with the promise of full scholarship and opportunities to study in prestigious institutions.

In addition, these universities and their local agents mount attractive marketing fairs throughout the Caribbean, to which students and parents are invited, sometimes through the auspices of education ministries. The lure of full scholarships, the core issue within aggressive marketing strategies, has been enormously effective. As previously noted, it has been said that US universities often annually appropriate the top performers of the Caribbean high school system, students who at an earlier time would have been destined for UWI.

While UK universities have taken aggressively to promoting a domestic "overseas students" market and to developing this sector as a major business operation that brings in millions of pounds in tuition fees, in the United States, the primary emphasis has been upon meeting the ethnic and gender quotas set out by state and federal legislatures.

The Competitive Market

The effect, however, is that all social classes within the Caribbean are targeted by foreign universities through scholarships and seductive media campaigns. In addition to these scholarships offered by globalizing universities, a range of other study-abroad financial packages are available to Caribbean students by the Organization of American States, the Association of Commonwealth Universities, the Japanese Development Bank Scholarship Programme, and the Governments of the United Kingdom, Canada, India, Israel, Mexico and the Netherlands.

Third, and this trend is rapidly growing in intensity, globalizing foreign universities are teaming up with Caribbean tertiary level institutions in order to sell to nationals a range of foreign programmes. Community colleges and private higher education institutions have benefited from this relationship in the offering of associate degrees as well as bachelor's and master's degrees. An effect of this global joint venturing is the creation of greater choice, if not widening access, by the building of capacity through resource sharing.

Unplanned Developments

Much concern, however, has been expressed in some quarters about the seemingly unplanned nature of these developments. There has not always been sufficient public debate and the feeling is that the issue of quality assurance has not always been kept at the centre. It has been said, for instance, that ACTI, as a family of tertiary level institutions, has served to facilitate the globalizing agendas of foreign universities with respect to penetrating the Caribbean catchment.

This argument cannot be sustained, however, as the tertiary level institutions have done very well in making their maximum contributions to the regional mandate of widening and expanding access, especially among non-traditional students. They have found these joint ven-

[All social classes within the Caribbean are targeted by foreign universities through scholarships and seductive media campaigns]

[An effect of this global joint venturing is the creation of greater choice, if not widening access, by the building of capacity through resource sharing]

ture relationships very productive and have shown how they can be put to sustainable development purposes.

Furthest ahead along this trajectory, and among the oldest participants, are the tertiary level institutions in the Bahamas and the British Virgin Islands. The College of the Bahamas has long had direct links with many US universities, and offshore ones locally, in offering a wide range of programmes. The H. Lavity Stoutt Community College in the British Virgin Islands has moved ahead with respect to establishing a joint venture with a New York company to distribute distance education from well-known US universities via high-speed Internet links. The college also has articulation agreements with the State University of New York at Buffalo and Wright State.

External Links

[As the tertiary level institutions and UWI are learning rapidly how to engage in collective planning in order to effectively re-engineer the regional higher education landscape]

In Barbados, the Samuel Jackman Prescod Polytechnic has links with the University of Wisconsin in the area of occupational health safety, and the Barbados Institute of Management and Productivity, a private institution, has teamed up with universities in the United States, United Kingdom and Singapore to deliver diploma programmes in management studies and MBAs.

There are offshore medical universities in St Lucia, St Vincent, St Kitts, Nevis, Saba, Dominica and Grenada. Jamaica has welcomed on shore Nova Southeastern University, Florida State University and the University of New Orleans from the United States, as well as the University of Wales and the University of Manchester from the United Kingdom, which are working in collaboration with the Jamaica Institute of Bankers. St Kitts currently hosts the Eastern Caribbean University, Ross University School of Veterinary Medicine, Windsor University of the Americas and the International University of the Health Sciences.

A Need for Planning

[Higher education can be globally industrialized and converted into a billion-dollar sector]

As the tertiary level institutions and UWI are learning rapidly how to engage in collective planning in order to effectively re-engineer the regional higher education landscape, the simultaneous mass entry of globalizing foreign universities, oftentimes with UWI being ill informed and unaware, has generated some suspicion and anxiety. At present, the major tertiary providers in the region cannot speak with certainty about each other's plans, and a lurking sense of resource competition and caution serves to tinge inter-institutional relations.

Globalization of the tertiary sector has been made possible and effective in large measure because of rapid developments in new information and communications technology. The recognition that higher education can be globally industrialized and converted into a billion-dollar sector has to do with its growing inclusion into agreed packages of civil rights.

Citizens in democracies are demanding access to the market economy process that is driven by trade liberalization, privatization and post–cold war Western financial and corporate expansion. Virtual technology has allowed globalizing universities to bring their programmes to Caribbean students, while political economy forces in North America have propelled institutions to simultaneously "import" young Caribbean students. This two-tiered development is having a telling effect on the local education market that was once monopolized by UWI.

The Caribbean Challenge

The physical and political environment within which UWI functions presents it with enormous potential to exploit the opportunities provided by globalization, particularly on account of the new information and communications technologies. As a knowledge centre within the economic South of the sociopolitical West, UWI is well placed to view and interact with Internet technologies, and, in the process, promote and facilitate regional networking with respect to educational globalization.

In addition, UWI is challenged to engage these forces of education globalization by illustrating to the region how best to extract value from the base line principles of trading liberalization, commercial privatization and the economic explosion associated with the marketing of intellectual properties rights. In short, the effective connection of UWI to the globalized economic systems of knowledge-ware can constitute a reliable and dynamic portal through which its stakeholders may venture with confidence.

The first step, however, will entail a revolutionary transformation of the very limited community access to Internet technologies, both with respect to educational communications and commercial enterprise. The United Nations Development Programme has projected that by the year 2001 more than seven hundred million people will have direct access to the Internet making it the "fastest-growing tool of communication ever". But Caribbean access to the Internet is tragically low, with less than 2 per cent of the population in effective use, despite its close proximity to the United States where 30 per cent of the population has direct access.

The principal constraints upon Caribbean Internet access can be found within the context of its low enrolment ratios in higher and tertiary education. With less than 15 per cent of the age cohort meaningfully engaged in this sector of the educational system, the anglophone Caribbean community is faced with the serious danger of experiencing persistent info-poverty during the first half of this century. Globally, the relationship between Internet access and higher educational enrolment is clear and direct: some 40 per cent of world users are graduates of higher education institutions; the ratio reaches as high as 55 per cent in the United Kingdom and 65 per cent in China.

Low Tertiary Enrolment

Low tertiary education enrolment ratios within UWI's catchment also serve to suppress considerably the natural, endemic advantages that should accrue to the community. English is the predominant Internet language, and it is used on over 78 per cent of the Web sites for both educational instruction and graphic displays. The evidence, which shows that only about 12 per cent of the world's populations are native speakers of English, reveals the extent of Caribbean marginalization and that non-native speakers of English dominate English-based Internet access.

In effect, then, the Caribbean cannot be described as a networked society, despite its great potential language advantage, largely because of its crisis of higher education access.

Internet Access

The United Nations Development Programme sets out seven clearly defined development objectives for the transformation of traditional societies (that is, those not invested with a sustainable electronic culture):

1. The region must be effectively connected to basic telecommunications and computer networks.

> [Within UWI itself, the Distance Education Programme and recent responses among students to Web-based self-instruction are telling indicators of the considerable gulf that exists between policy expectations and reality]

2. The approach to enhancing access must focus on communities and other large-scale organizations rather than individuals.

3. Higher education systems must promote the knowledge society at the level of core policy.

4. The knowledge content delivered and transmitted should be relevant, focusing on a high local input and output.

5. The bias in favour of indigenous content should be driven by the adaptation of the technologies to local user standards, taste and methods.

6. There should be effective promotion of global collaboration so that the principles of sharing and collective creativity are given extensive opportunities for expression.

7. The entire exercise should feature stakeholder approaches to the domestic generation of funds to sustain access.

Internet Distress

It would seem that, at present, most societies principally served by UWI are some distance away from attaining these objectives. Only an enormous policy initiative, scientifically and rigorously implemented, can be effective in turning around the increasingly negative trend. Within UWI itself, the Distance Education Programme and recent responses among students to Web-based self-instruction are telling indicators of the considerable gulf that exists between policy expectations and reality as lived.

For over a decade, UWI's policy makers recognized that distance learning through audio conferencing was the key modality for revolutionizing access at relatively lower cost to university programmes. Fortunately, the development of a reliable regional telecommunications infrastructure assisted the institution in building capability to pursue non-campus learning solutions. Shortly thereafter UWI declared itself a dual-mode operation and moved to deliver parts of most programmes by distance.

> [UWI declared itself a dual-mode operation and moved to deliver parts of most programmes by distance]

While the challenge of developing relevant course content and strong staff support was effectively conceived, inadequate budget allocations meant that the distance learning programme suffered at the outset. In addition, difficulties and constraints associated with an undeveloped electronic and cyber community, institutional management inertia and

> [They perceived distance teaching as an "add-on" rather than a core part of their work]

the conservatism of a mostly traditionally trained teaching faculty aggravated this condition.

Resisting Change

In effect, UWI became a dual-mode institution with single-mode management and faculty, and with students whose cultural bias remains attached to the traditional pre-electronic classroom. Research surveys among teaching faculty, for example, confirmed the general perception that they perceived distance teaching as an "add-on" rather than a core part of their work.

The attempt by the Faculty of Social Sciences at Mona to teach its foundation course by Web-based self-instruction in academic year 1999/2000 led to massive student resistance on the grounds that they were ill prepared for the innovation, both in their pre-university education and by the faculties in which they were enroled.

This failed attempt to create a teaching niche in which to develop the electronic culture speaks to the wider forms of cultural and administrative preparation that are required in order to facilitate the effective use of new information and communications technologies in education. That academies such as Middlesex University in the United Kingdom only communicate with their students via email indicates how far UWI is away from embracing intimately these technologies.

[Academies such as Middlesex University in the United Kingdom only communicate with their students via email]

E-Training

Some progress is being made, however, with respect to interactive learning technologies for faculties. The Mona campus has joined with VILCOMM (a private technology business) to offer training to members of staff in many multimedia technologies. The Infocom Centre, located in the Department of Computer Sciences, began training in June 2000. It is reported that nearly one hundred members of staff have participated in the training programmes. Several workshops have been conducted since then and there is ongoing training in the following areas:

- Multimedia presentations – digital writing, imaging and video; basic animation; and CD-ROM archiving

- Collaboration tools – chat zones; electronic whiteboard; audio and video conferencing; Web-browsers collaboration software.

At Cave Hill there are no specific plans to offer training in Web-based teaching. The campus is about to employ the personnel who would incorporate the new technologies into the wider computer-based training programmes, and there are facilities and resources in place when this gets started.

At St Augustine the only campus-wide technology training that is being carried out is in the area of Microsoft Office software. Individual members of staff have been learning to design Web-based courses. The Faculty of Social Sciences Software Training 2000 is offering some training in this area, but there are no specific training programmes that target faculty members.

Building High-Touch

Resource and cultural constraints at this time mean that UWI has been unable to project itself aggressively into the high-touch technology end of the education market. Instead, it has had to rely on its traditional strengths in order to remain a major player in the delivery race. But these traditional strengths are consistently being undermined and diminished on account of the institution receiving inadequate, change-promoting inputs such as innovative electronic-based pedagogy and curricula.

In the end the question of quality will be the deciding factor and increasing the concept is being defined in terms of effective access to these technologies. Students in a globalized education market will vote with their feet, and there is every reason to believe that they take cyber-driven quality very seriously in choosing a university that will be their temporary home and permanent intellectual enabler.

Education Liberalization

Most Caribbean governments, it seems, welcome globalizing interventions. Few have examined the quality implication for the tertiary sector, or the impact upon effective long-term planning of the sector with respect to the survival of fledgling national tertiary level institutions, not to mention UWI, the University of Technology (Jamaica) and the University of Guyana. Recently, however, the Government of Jamaica has called for such an examination as part of its knowledge base with respect to decision making regarding the funding of UWI.

These universities enjoy amicable relations with host governments, as is particularly evident in the supportive statements made by ministers of government at their graduation exercises and other occasions. From this, it ought to be clear that the political thinking across the region is that globalizing foreign universities, both by coming to students and importing students, have a critical role to play in the regional human resource development strategy.

[Most Caribbean governments, it seems, welcome these globalizing interventions]

Expectations of Outside Influence

As such, a new higher education system is rapidly coming into place, with national institutions challenged to compete and to distinguish themselves against the performance of globalizing foreign universities. On close examination, furthermore, it appears that some regional governments expect these resource-rich foreign institutions to revolutionize the national tertiary sector by exposing it to advanced virtual teaching and learning technology.

There are now nearly one hundred foreign universities operating within the anglophone CARICOM region that has a mere three national universities. The phenomenon of the aggressively globalizing North Atlantic university is being felt throughout the tertiary sector of developing countries. In both its physical and virtual manifestation these institutions are participating in the refashioning of the education discourse in Africa, Asia, Latin America, the Middle East and eastern Europe.

[A new higher education system is rapidly coming into place, with national institutions challenged to compete and to distinguish themselves against the performance of globalizing foreign universities]

View from the "South"

The subject has drawn sufficient reaction from educators and other education stakeholders to warrant a special pioneering conference, which was convened in Cape Town, South Africa in March 2001 under the title "Globalization and Higher Education: Views from the South". Conference organizers noted that not all parts of the South are experiencing this process in the same way, and both negative and positive effects must be assessed and debated.

[There are now nearly one hundred foreign universities operating within the anglophone CARICOM region that has a mere three national universities]

[Not all parts of the South are experiencing this process in the same way]

The conference aims to:
- provide an international forum for critically investigating the implications of globalization on higher education, particularly from the perspective of the South and less industrialized countries across the globe;
- deepen our knowledge of the variety of higher education systems in transition in countries and subregions of the less industrialized countries, including both anglophone and non-
- anglophone countries;
- extend our knowledge at a global level, of the interrelationships of higher education systems between advanced industrialized countries and lesser industrialized countries in the light of globalization; and
- strengthen the network of higher education scholars globally to facilitate the development of teaching and research in the field of higher education studies, especially but not exclusively in the South and Asia

This international conference was hosted jointly by the Education Policy Unit of the University of the Western Cape in Cape Town, South Africa, a research unit specializing in higher education policy analysis, and the Society for Research into Higher Education. It was also organized in association with the Association of Commonwealth Universities.

UWI's Strategic Responses

[UWI has not gone global with its academic products as a strategic response to the global industrialization of higher education]

Despite having a well-established worldwide network of graduates, supporters and admirers, UWI has not gone global with its academic product as a strategic response to the global industrialization of higher education. In this sense, then, it can be said that the institution has not cashed in fully on its enormous international intellectual capital. Financial necessity is privileging this possibility and UWI stakeholders expected it to respond appropriately. UWI now has the opportunity to market its academic capability, which was never questioned.

At the level of public policy, UWI is expected to further its reach within the wider CARIFORUM region and to become a major provider in the non-anglophone cultures. Already some important initiatives with the Dominican Republic are proving effective and valuable. The logical first step has therefore been conceived and taken. What is required at this stage is aggressive special-initiative expansion and consolidation.

✧ *Diaspora Expansion*

The time is also right for UWI to take its programmes beyond CARIFORUM into the North Atlantic region where it has accumulated a comparative advantage in many disciplinary areas. And it must do so in a way that suggests a well-thought-out counterinitiative and a new approach in its own tradition of academic internationalization rather than as a part of the growing phenomenon of neo-imperial education globalization. Its credibility and expertise are well known and enduring, built as they are upon a proven history of relevance and quality.

There is already a significant comparative advantage within the context of the rapidly expanding and endemic demand for Caribbean studies. We know this because, despite the existence of Caribbean studies centres throughout the United States and Europe, for example, UWI is still regarded as the premier institution in the world for Caribbean studies. Indeed, it has been said that these metropolitan centres have emerged partly as a result of UWI's conservatism and refusal to capture the Caribbean studies initiative in the face of an obvious demand.

Packaging Knowledge

New information and communications technologies give UWI a fair opportunity to offer its teaching programmes and partner research agendas in disciplines such as law, medicine, the social sciences, marine biology, theology, cultural arts and the humanities. By combining on-site delivery with distance and Internet access, UWI can offer degree programmes within and beyond the diaspora. It can do so on a stand-alone basis or in partnership with European and US universities. In addition to degree programmes at the bachelor's and master's levels, it can also mount special summer school and accredited semester packages.

A paradigm shift has taken place in the regional tertiary sector which, if not effectively managed and responded to strategically, will not serve the interest of the region and its peoples. The future clearly speaks to the need for greater openness within the sector, but it also calls for an assertion of a more pertinent, restructured Caribbean identity and academic self-sufficiency. These two circumstances combined tell us that the guiding principle in the years ahead should be "planned openness and diversity". The challenge, therefore, is for UWI to respond strategically by improving the quality of all its academic programmes and administrative machinery and preparing for its first truly international initiative.

8 Collaboration or Competition?

[UWI simply cannot satisfy the market because it is severely restricted in the number of students it can accept each year]

It is evident that UWI alone cannot at this time meet the demand for higher education in the region. UWI simply cannot satisfy the market because it is severely restricted in the number of students it can accept each year. In this regard, the role of other state-run tertiary level institutions and private providers is vital.

This realization, however, has not reduced the interest of many students who consider UWI as the leading higher education institution in the subregion, and a place they would wish to go. The financial and physical limits of UWI have not gone unnoticed either by the local tertiary level institutions or by foreign universities.

[The financial and physical limits of UWI have not gone unnoticed]

Responsiveness

Competition with UWI for potential students is seen as coming from extra-regional institutions as well as regional tertiary level institutions. It is said, for example, that overseas universities, in the United Kingdom and the United States in particular, are far more responsive to the needs of persons who wish to work while studying. Working adults who seek alternatives to traditional forms of delivery of degree level courses are turning also to those local providers who have formed strategic alliances with overseas institutions.

[When UWI is reluctant to offer credits for courses taken through other providers, foreign universities and professional bodies often seem keener to do so]

When UWI is reluctant to offer credits for courses taken through other providers, foreign universities and professional bodies often seem keener to do so. Many training institutions, especially those offering business and computer courses, have been carving out their niche here. It is noted that UWI is either unwilling or too slow to respond to the requests for collaboration and, as a result, private schools and other colleges turn their attention to non-national institutions.

A Simpler System

It is therefore not surprising that critics of UWI focus on notions such as its alleged elitism, rigidity in matriculation requirements and slowness to change to the demands of the education market. Many prospective students are attracted by the more liberal entry requirements and credit mobility of other regional and foreign institutions.

There is also a perception that too many complexities exist in the way linkages are made between other institutions and UWI. But with the establishment with UWI of the Tertiary Level Institutions Unit, more tertiary level institutions are seeking, and being granted, articulation agreements with UWI.

[Many prospective students are attracted by the more liberal entry requirements and credit mobility of other regional and foreign institutions]

Losing the Edge

Aggressive recruitment strategies by colleges and universities in the United States are attracting large numbers of science students. Most recently, almost all the science students from one high school in Jamaica were accepted to US colleges and universities, most of them with full financial aid, on the basis of their CXC results and their performance on the SAT. They did not have to wait for A levels. Those who remain enter the fierce competition for places at UWI, especially in the professional faculties of engineering and medicine.

Extra-regional institutions are able to enter the region and, in conjunction with local and regional institutions, recruit a sizeable number of students who wish to access higher education but find UWI either too expensive or restrictive.

[Almost all the science students from one high school in Jamaica were accepted to US colleges and universities, most of them with full financial aid]

✣ Areas of Interest

The most popular programmes that are available in a variety of delivery modes are in business studies. These courses are in addition to the professional programmes offered through local and regional institutions by the Association of Chartered Certified Accountants, the Chartered Institute of Marketing, the Association of Business Executives and the Association of Accounting Technicians. Nova Southeastern University has carved out a significant niche in the market in the Bahamas and Jamaica by offering online master's in business administration and human resource management.

[The most popular programmes made available in a variety of delivery modes are in business]

Further, the popularity of Nova Southeastern University's postgraduate programmes in Jamaica has encouraged its expansion into undergraduate degree programmes. The Bachelor of Professional Management is now perceived to be the first stage of the progression to other master's programmes offered by Nova Southeastern University.

Greater Choice

It is in Trinidad and Tobago, however, where there is a much wider scope for students who wish to take courses in business and computing that articulate into degree programmes of foreign universities. The work of three institutions in Trinidad and Tobago is worth highlighting: Royal Bank Institute of Business and Technology, the School of Business and Computer Science, and the School of Accounting and Management.

The Royal Bank Institute of Business and Technology, situated in the heart of Port of Spain, offers business seminars in conjunction with international and local partners. In-house training and consulting interventions constitute a strong part of the work of the Royal Bank Institute of Business and Technology in the region.

Through the American Management Association, the Royal Bank Institute of Business and Technology offers a one-year Certificate in Management. Its academic programmes include:

- Associate of Arts in Journalism and Media Arts
- Associate of Science in Information Systems Management (articulation agreement with Munroe College, New York)
- Associate of Science in Management (leading to a Bachelor of Business Administration)
- Bachelor of Education degree for primary school teachers (via distance)

Thinking Business

The School of Business and Computer Science, located almost directly opposite the Faculty of Medical Sciences (St Augustine) at Mount Hope, has as part of its philosophy "to reflect the imperatives of tomorrow's environment with its new technologies, globalization of markets and world wide". Its programmes include:

[There is a much wider scope for students who wish to take courses in business and computing that articulate into degree programmes of foreign universities]

- Bachelor of Law (with the University of London)
- Bachelor of Science in Management (University of London)
- Bachelor of Science in Information Systems and Management (University of London)
- Bachelor of Science (Honours) in Computing (University of Greenwich)
- Bachelor of Science in Computing and Information Systems (University of London)
- Diploma in Computing and Information Systems (University of London)
- Bachelor of Engineering (Honours) (University of Sunderland)

The School of Accounting and Management in St Augustine, Trinidad, offers wide undergraduate degree programmes in international business, accounting, and computing and information systems. The School of Accounting and Management is a representative of the Canadian-based Certificate in General Accounting. Students are given the option of obtaining a Bachelor of Accounting Science from the University of Calgary by studying for only four subjects after completing Stage 4 of the Certificate in General Accounting.

The strengths of the School of Accounting and Management lie, it is suggested, in its emphasis on distance education using state-of-the-art technologies and credit transfers and/or exemptions. The programmes have many attractive features, such as fees that include textbooks, computer software, video and cassette tapes and the school encourages mature student entry.

[The strengths of the School of Accounting and Management lie ...in its emphasis on distance education using state-of-the-art technologies and credit transfers and/or exemptions]

Market Requirements

Leaders in the private sector have noted that the more reputable training institutions in the region understand the working environment. These institutions have established successful partnerships with foreign universities and professional bodies, and, by doing so, they attract students who would have gone to UWI. Despite their relatively short time in the business, the private schools of accounting, management and computing have established reputations that are spreading among employees in industry, commerce and the public sector.

[They offer attractive alternatives because of the flexibility of academic programming]

> [They are prepared to make the sacrifice because the extra-regional universities give them a quality opportunity]

Some regional institutions have been successful, it is said, because they utilize the expertise of practitioners and the students can make the link between theory and practice through this experience. They offer attractive alternatives because of the flexibility of academic programming, especially those developed through CD-ROMs, online tutors, online libraries and Internet connection.

Extra-regional institutions and their regional partners embrace the new information and communications technologies and provide valuable links with the community of the working student. Students who access these programmes will say, however, that while costs can be higher than similar programmes at UWI, they are prepared to make the sacrifice because the extra-regional universities give them a quality opportunity.

Making and Using Links

Many public and private providers of higher education and training indicate that they would much prefer doing business with UWI through articulation agreements, transfer credits or joint delivery of programmes. They recognize that UWI has an outstanding track record, especially in the quality of its graduates in medicine, engineering and law.

> [UWI has an outstanding track record especially in the quality of its graduates in medicine, engineering and law]

However, accessing UWI's professional faculties through any route other than traditional A levels is a major hurdle for mature students, even if they have highly valued experience outside the formal higher education system. These students are embraced not only by national institutions but also by foreign colleges and universities who give credits for such experience.

It is widely believed that a market-driven philosophy is not yet a core part of the ethos of UWI. It is believed that the concern at UWI is more about the quality of those who seek entry than about the type and relevance of its programmes, especially in management studies, accountancy, computing and information systems. This is one area of strength of both regional and external providers of degree-level programmes.

Joint Ventures

Some national and regional institutions, however, now act as facilitators for extra-regional universities, providing space and local tutors; others collaborate in curriculum development of courses and modules. There has been much concern expressed, primarily in Trinidad and Tobago, that large amounts of foreign exchange leave the country for course and examination fees and the payment of the expenses of visiting lecturers and administrators.

It is clear that even students without scholarships are not turned off by the costs and financial challenges associated with meeting the requirements of non-regional universities. Some institutions like Nova Southeastern University and the University of New Orleans arrange financial aid packages for their students facilitated by regional financial institutions. Added benefits such as a laptop computer and online access to their libraries reduce students' concerns about high tuition fees.

Medicine and Allied Health Disciplines

Affiliated or otherwise, offshore medical schools see the Caribbean as uncharted territory. The numbers seem to be growing and students who have realized that anything less than three good A levels in the sciences may not be effective in securing a place in UWI's medical schools may seek entry into these offshore schools, greater costs notwithstanding.

The University of Health Sciences in Antigua, is an offshore medical school that has begun to accept Antiguans into its programmes. As mentioned in chapter 7, the University of Wisconsin, in association with the Samuel Jackman Prescod Polytechnic (Barbados), offers occupational health safety. St Matthew's University School of Medicine operates in Belize. St George's University has expanded its medical school and has established a campus – the Kingstown Medical College – in St Vincent and the Grenadines.

In September 2000 a new Medical University of the Americas campus opened in Charlestown, Nevis, taking in thirty-five students drawn from Lebanon, the United States, Canada and Nevis. There are others whose reputation is not readily known. But to the less discriminating who can pay, any opportunity to gain entry into medical school is welcomed.

The expansive web of education, helped by new information and communications technologies, is reaching the shores of the Caribbean at a rate few fully fathom. UWI might have history and excellence on its side, but reputation alone will not deter its competitors. It must redefine itself as more than an alternative. UWI has to show that access to programmes is not blocked by systems and bureaucracy, nor discouraged by outmoded teaching and learning methodologies. It must reach beyond its western horizons, utilizing the very mechanisms and strategies that extra-regional entities use to bring more students into the higher education experience.

Coming for the Best

[People in the North Atlantic, especially, view West Indian culture as profoundly sophisticated]

It has become clear that Caribbean cultural creativity, demonstrated through excellence in music, dance, food and art, is not afflicted by pessimism and negativity. Upon closer examination of the region's cultural expressions, it has been recognized that people in the North Atlantic, especially, view West Indian culture as profoundly sophisticated.

The West Indies produces excellent students at all levels of the system, an achievement to be celebrated when consideration is given to the amount of money spent on education. Institutions in the United Kingdom, Canada and the United States have begun to target these students as early as Grade 9. They recognize that these students can help to consolidate their academic reputation.

Recruiting Quality

[The West Indies produces excellent students at all levels of the system, an achievement to be celebrated when consideration is given to the amount of money spent on education]

While the external motivation for West Indians to study abroad is great there is a significant "push factor". Guidance counsellors and recruitment agents provide strong arguments for why studying abroad is an attractive option; but competition for places in national and regional higher education institutions is fierce.

Recruitment officers in the United States are well aware of the challenges facing secondary students trying to get into UWI and the University of Technology, for example. Notwithstanding cultural biases in the SAT tests, local individuals and institutions introduce students to these tests even in Grade 9. If the student gets a "good" score in the SAT then colleges and universities will send them the entry information.

Scholarship Market

As for their US high school counterparts, the effort then begins to access scholarships. One Jamaican agent has developed an outstanding reputation for being able to secure scholarships for students. Parents are encouraged to assist their children in getting into US colleges and universities. Some students are now openly discouraged from applying to UWI. In many cases, students are advised to wait a year if scholarships are not available after Sixth Form rather than enter UWI.

North Americans recognize the benefits to be derived from an education system that produces outstanding students at all levels. Thus they pursue the students who graduate with honours and offer them lucrative postgraduate scholarships. Finally, they have begun to recruit our teachers.

Traditions of External Access

The region has always been attractive to foreign employers. Nurses, farmers and workers in the hotel industry are considered reliable and hardworking. The migration of graduates and professionals is also worth noting. The harsh reality is that, on balance, globalization is having an adverse effect on the region.

Within this context, and with limited resources provided for education, the region manages to do well, at least according to the United Nations. Traditionally, the typical West Indian migrant was a farm or factory worker; today, he or she is more likely to be a student or teacher.

Summary

As the twenty-first century opens, educators can see more clearly that the society our youth will inhabit will be shaped by the growing importance of knowledge as the key force in economic development and social transformation. Higher education in particular, as one of the main pillars of globalization, will assume even greater importance as the most powerful force in determining the level at which citizens will participate in economic and civil society activities.

Caribbean people today are as much at the centre of postmodern discourses about development as they were primary witnesses at the onset of modernity. They are experiencing this phase of globalization with an intensity that suggests familiarity with earlier stages. The arena of higher education is a principal site where this process can be seen and heard with greatest clarity.

[Caribbean people today are as much at the centre of post-modern discourses about development as they were primary witnesses at the onset of modernity]

Effects of Globalization

The transforming effect of globalization in the education sector is a major feature of the new social reality in the Caribbean. It is as divisive of the popular imagination as it is integrating of the public opportunities. In the region the demand for higher education has outstripped its capacity to deliver. Additional access can be secured through migration to the North Atlantic or by enrolment in offshore universities registered in the region. Development requires the building of regional capacity and the retention of trained human resources. But the availability of a variety of educational opportunities for citizens can only serve the region in a positive way.

In all instances, consumers of the higher education product are seeking quality, at home and beyond. They expect to enrol in programmes that are relevant, opportunity creating and cost effective. This is as much a market expectation as a civil right. As the average age of students in

[The transforming effect of globalization in the education sector is a major feature of the new social reality in the Caribbean. It is as divisive of the popular imagination as it is integrating of the public opportunities]

the region's institutions continue to rise away from the teens, reflecting the growing relative demand of working adults, the planning approaches of these institutions have begun to shift from operations to a student-centred culture.

A Caribbean Response

A key realization in this transition is that UWI and the other tertiary level institutions are expected to respond effectively to fulfil the national purposes for which they have been created. The economic and social positioning of universities in the development discourse is therefore a vital issue, particularly for developing countries where resources for higher education are diminishing in many instances.

UWI is experiencing all of the stresses and strains of the postmodern university within a developing society. It has been transformed from an elite university catering for the few to a mass university with open access, distance modes and online delivery. Enrolment has doubled over the past decade, and this with less than matching financial resources. At the same time, it has been charged with maintaining its high quality and standards in order to be internationally respected and competitive. This is a normal landscape; to date, the results have been impressive, and largely because of the insistence upon quality within the academic and management cultures.

> [UWI is experiencing all of the stresses and strains of the postmodern university within a developing society]

Inadequate Access

But despite the considerable expansion of enrolment, the region still has good reason to be concerned that access to higher education in general is inadequate for the youth cohort targeted as agents of development. The region still feels the adverse effects of a shortage of effective human resources in many vital areas, a circumstance that places even greater responsibility upon the university to find answers by working in partnership with other institutions of higher education.

Since it is clear that access to quality higher education is the most important force for the achievement of new strategies of development, the capacity to domesticate the new information and communications technologies within the academy will determine not only the quality of programmes but whether UWI's reputation will survive. By focusing

> [But despite the considerable expansion of enrolment, the region still has good reason to be concerned that access to higher education in general is inadequate for the youth cohort targeted as agents of development]

[The framework used in UWI in its quality assurance procedures and mechanisms is therefore designed to transform rather than reform]

upon the role of new information and communications technologies in the quality revolution, UWI has embarked upon a process of redefining policies, plans, curricula and management capacity with a commitment to creative innovation and broad-based transformation.

The Quality Revolution

The quality revolution at UWI is essentially a consensual strategy because the point has been grasped that it is better for such a process to emerge from within the academy than be imposed by the market or the criticisms of external stakeholders. The challenge of the quality assurance drive, then, is to reinvent UWI in order to remove its recognized deficiencies and rise to meet the new demands of Caribbean society by preserving its wealth of traditions, cultural values, creativity and diversity.

The framework used in UWI in its quality assurance procedures and mechanisms is therefore designed to transform rather than reform. By centring students within the discourse, ensuring the academic autonomy of faculties and focusing upon the empowerment of the teacher-student relationship, the framework has proven to be effective and efficient. In this regard, UWI is well on the way to developing, with all relevant partners, a comprehensive vision of its goals, tasks and functioning.

Appendix 1

Selected Tertiary Education Quality Assurance Systems

Europe

Experts in quality assurance reviews and audit have shown the following features of national evaluation systems now established in western Europe:

- Governments have generally adopted a hands-off approach (that is, the quality assurance agencies generally have considerable freedom of operation and in setting up relevant procedures and methodologies).

- The central purposes are accountability to stakeholders and improvement.

- The outcomes of evaluation do not confer a status (that is, the outcomes do not lead to accreditation, and usually there is no link between the outcomes and government funding).

- Evaluations are based on the missions and goals stated by the institutions and on the stated aims and objectives of programmes.

- Checks are made to follow up which actions institutions take on the evaluation reports.

- Academic staff have slowly come to accept that evaluation is necessary and can be beneficial.

- International collaboration is increasing.

- The results of evaluations are publicly reported.

Despite the similarity in these broad features, there are differences in detail about the agencies: their legal status, governance, funding, number of permanent staff and so on; the focus of their evaluations; their selection and training of peers; the length of site visits and the methods used during these visits; and the style and confidentiality of their reports.

United Kingdom

There are over 180 universities and colleges of higher education in the United Kingdom with the oldest being over eight hundred years old. These institutions cover a wide range of activity, have varied backgrounds and have student enrolment ranging from 120 to 200,000. There are also higher education programmes within some 270 further education colleges. It is the responsibility of each institution to offer a good quality education and to ensure that appropriate standards are achieved. In a higher education system that caters for mass participation, prospective students, parents and employers all need clear information about courses and qualifications. Employers want to know what they can expect from graduates who are candidates for jobs and have expressed a need for greater explicitness and clarity about standards and the levels of achievement required for different awards.

New Institution

The Quality Assurance Agency (QAA) was established in 1997 following a 1996 recommendation for a single agency to rationalize the processes then in operation. The QAA provides assurance that quality and standards within higher education institutions are being safeguarded and enhanced. Reviews are conducted by teams, most of whom are academics, but with some members drawn, where appropriate, from industry, commerce and the professions. Prior to 1997 there were three systems of external scrutiny of higher education in the United Kingdom:

- academic quality audit – a process of review of institutions' academic quality assurance mechanisms – established by the universities in the late 1980s;

- teaching quality assessment by the Higher Education Funding Councils for the United Kingdom, the bodies that provided financial support to most institutions (the funding councils had a statutory responsibility to assess the quality of education that they funded to ensure that public money was not wasted on unsatisfactory programmes); and

- accreditation by professional and statutory bodies of programmes of study that lead to a professional title (for example, the General

Medical Council accredits programmes leading to registration to practise medicine) – this type of accreditation ensures that a programme of study provides sufficient of the competencies needed for professional practice.

Review Culture

The QAA has at its core the business of reviewing the quality and standards of higher education in the United Kingdom to promote public confidence in higher education. It is an independent body funded by subscriptions from universities and colleges of higher education and through contracts with the main higher education funding bodies. The QAA audits the universities' and colleges' management of the quality and standards of their provision and reviews academic standards and the quality of teaching and learning in subject areas. The QAA has published a code of practice for the assurance of academic quality and standards in higher education, national frameworks for higher education qualifications, statements of subject benchmark standards and a framework for programme specification. These provide public information about higher education in the United Kingdom and are reference points for the reviews. Further, the reports of reviews and audits are available to the public and this information is helpful to prospective students and their advisers, when applications are made to universities and colleges. It may be used also by employers who recruit graduates, and by those professional and regulatory bodies that recognize higher education awards that count towards their qualifications.

Review Process

Qualification frameworks for the United Kingdom have been developed by the QAA and are designed to make it easier to understand higher education qualifications by ensuring consistent use of qualification titles. They promote a clearer understanding of the achievements and attributes represented by the titles such as bachelor's degree with honours, master's degree and doctorate. By setting out the attributes and abilities that can be expected of the holder of a qualification, the frameworks help students and employers understand the meaning and level of qualifications. They also provide public assurance that qualifications bearing similar titles represent similar levels of achievement.

Subject benchmark statements set out expectations about standards of degrees in broad subject areas. They concern the conceptual framework that gives a discipline its coherence and identity, and they define what can be expected of a graduate in terms of the techniques and skills needed for understanding in the subject. They are benchmarks of the level of intellectual demand and challenge represented by a degree in the subject area concerned. The benchmark statements are intended to help higher education institutions when they design and approve programmes. The statements help external examiners and academic reviewers to verify and compare standards and also provide information for students and employers.

Specification Concept

Programme specifications are standard sets of information that each institution provides about its programmes. Each specification clarifies what knowledge, understanding, skills and other attributes a student will have developed on successfully completing a specific programme. It also provides details of teaching and learning methods, assessment, and subsequent career opportunities and sets out how the programme relates to the qualifications framework. This information allows prospective students to make comparisons and informed choices about the programmes they wish to study and provides useful guidance for recruiters of graduates.

Code of Practice

The *Code of Practice* sets out guidelines on good practice relating to the management of academic quality and standards. Each section of the *Code of Practice* has precepts or principles that institutions should demonstrate, together with guidance on how they might meet these precepts. Sections cover postgraduate research programmes; collaborative provision; students with disabilities; external examining; academic appeals and student complaints on academic matters; assessment of students; programme approval; monitoring and review; and career education, information and guidance.

The QAA also audits academic partnerships with overseas colleges that offer teaching leading to the award of degrees from UK institutions. These audits assess how effectively the UK institution manages both the maintenance of standards of its awards in its overseas programmes and the quality of those programmes.

Accreditation Bodies

In recent years the QAA has worked closely with the higher education sector to develop and introduce an integrated system of review called academic review. Professional and statutory bodies continue to accredit academic programmes for the purpose of granting licences to practise in the fields for which they are responsible, but much of the evidence they need for this is now drawn from the QAA reviews. Academic review is the QAA integrated method of review that focuses on the establishment, maintenance and enhancement of quality and academic standards. It operates over a six-year cycle, with each institution and all subjects being reviewed once in each cycle.

The academic review process addresses three interdependent areas:

- reporting on academic standards – this is concerned with the appropriateness of the intended learning outcomes (in relation to relevant subject benchmark statements, the qualifications framework and the overall aims of provision), effectiveness of curriculum design and assessment arrangements (in relation to the intended learning outcomes), and the actual achievement of students;

- reporting on the quality of learning opportunities in a subject – this is concerned with the effectiveness of teaching, learning resources and academic support in promoting student learning and achievement; and

- reporting on institutional management of standards and quality – this is concerned with the robustness and security of processes and procedures relating to the institution's responsibility as a body able to grant degrees and other awards that have a national and international standing. It involves arrangements for dealing with approval and review of programmes, the management of academic credit and qualification arrangements and the management of assessment procedures.

Education Modes

The first two areas are addressed by reviews at subject level, the last by reviews at the level of the whole institution. In each case, a self-evaluation document is produced. This allows reflection on what it does, why and how (the methods it uses to fulfil its aims). A team of reviewers analyses the self-evaluation and then visits the institution to gather the evidence they need to make their judgements. For each subject area in an institution, a judgement is made about academic standards.

Reviewers consider whether:

- there are clear learning outcomes that have been set appropriately in relation to the qualifications framework and any relevant subject benchmark statements;

- the curriculum is designed to enable the intended outcomes to be achieved;

- assessment is effective in measuring achievement of the outcomes; and

- student achievement matches the intended outcomes and the level of the qualification.

Importance of Standards

In the light of these factors, reviewers state whether they have confidence in standards, limited confidence in standards or no confidence in standards.

For each subject area reviewed in an institution, judgements about the quality of learning opportunities offered to students are made against the broad aims of the provision and the intended learning outcomes of the programmes. Reviewers look at:

- effectiveness of teaching and learning in relation to curriculum content and programme aims;

- student progression – recruitment, academic support, progression within the programme; and

- learning resources – the adequacy and effectiveness of use of the library, equipment, accommodation and staff.

Each of these three categories is judged as commendable, approved or failing. Within the commendable category, reviewers identify any specific exemplary features that represent sector-leading best practice. If reviewers have no confidence in the standards achieved, or if they find that any aspect of quality of learning opportunities is failing, then the provision will be subject to a further formal review within a year.

UK Institutional Review

Institutional review addresses the ultimate responsibility for the management of quality and standards that rests with the institution as a whole. It is concerned particularly with the way an institution exercises its powers as a body able to grant degrees and other awards. For example, it looks at institutional procedures for approval, monitoring and review of academic programmes; procedures for acting on the findings of external examiners, subject reviews and other external scrutinies; overall management of assessment processes; overall management of credit systems; and management of collaborative arrangements with other institutions. The institutional review draws on the evidence of subject level reviews and uses points of reference provided by sections of the *Code of Practice*. Reports list action points that are categorized as essential, advisable or desirable.

Building Confidence

Judgements are made on the degree of confidence that may reasonably be placed in an institution's effectiveness in managing the academic standards of its awards and the quality of its programmes. A statement that confidence cannot be placed in institutional arrangements would result if there were several matters requiring essential action, the combined effect of which would render ineffective the quality assurance arrangements as a whole. A statement that limited confidence only could be placed in institutional arrangements might be made if there are a small number of "essential" action points that could readily be implemented, or a large number of "advisable" points. In all other cases there would be a statement of "overall confidence" in the institutional arrangements. The QAA then monitors closely the responses of institutions to "essential" action points.

Collaborative Review

Some higher education institutions in the United Kingdom franchise their programmes of study to partner organizations. They may also, as the awarding or "validating" institution, allow other organizations to design and provide programmes leading to qualifications that they award. The QAA reviews collaborative activity to establish how an institution assures the quality of programmes offered in its name by a partner organization and ensures that the academic standards of awards gained through study with partner organizations are the same as those gained through study with the institution itself. Sometimes collaborative activity can be reviewed effectively through the main institutional-level academic review.

United States

Accreditation

Accreditation is the process used education in the United States to ensure that schools, post-secondary institutions and other education providers meet and maintain minimum standards of quality and integrity regarding academic programmes, administration and related services. It is a voluntary process based on the principle of academic self-governance. Both institutions and faculties within institutions participate in accreditation processes. The entities that conduct accreditation are associations comprised of institutions and academic specialists in specific subjects who establish and enforce standards of membership and procedures for conducting the accreditation process.

Accreditation: The Key

Both the federal and state governments recognize accreditation as the mechanism by which institutional and programmatic legitimacy and capacity are measured. The Council on Higher Education Accreditation represents the US accrediting community responsible for setting post-secondary standards. It is involved in international and distance education issues as well as domestic quality assurance. The steps that must be followed in order for accreditation to be a legitimate process include:

1. The accrediting association establishes, and periodically refines, its standards and policies to be followed by all successful candidates for accreditation or re-accreditation.
2. An institution or faculty applies to the association for membership as an accredited entity or, if it is already a member, is notified that the time for re-accreditation has come.
3. The institution or faculty begins a process of preparing and conducting an intensive and thorough self-study following guidelines set forth by the accrediting association.
4. The accrediting association selects a team of external academic and administrative experts from other similar institutions/faculties. This team reviews the self-study report and then visits the institution, following the association's evaluation guidelines.
5. The evaluation team issues a report recommending for or against accreditation or re-accreditation, and enumerating any conditions that need to be met before full positive approval may be given.
6. The members of the accrediting association vote on the status of the candidate or member based on the evaluation team report.

Each accrediting association publishes its standards, policies and guidelines as well as official lists of candidates, members and re-accredited members. Information is also published on candidates denied accreditation and on members whose accreditation is made probationary or revoked.

Types of Accreditation

In the United States, *Regional Accrediting Associations* accredit institutions located within defined groups of states and territories, as well as foreign institutions located in specified countries and world regions that apply for accreditation in the United States. While regional associations inspect and approve all types of institutions, they particularly serve traditional institutions that offer degree programmes in a full range of academic subjects, such as universities and colleges. There are six regional accrediting associations.

National Accrediting Associations accredit institutions located anywhere and concentrate on providing accreditation to institutions offering degree programmes in a narrow range of related specialized subjects, or using non-traditional modes of delivery, rather than to comprehensive liberal arts institutions.

Professional or Specialized Accrediting Associations accredit specific programmes of study offered within and by institutions that are regionally or nationally accredited. Professional/specialized associations do not accredit entire institutions except in a few cases where an institution offers only one degree programme in a single subject, and thus accreditation of the programme is equivalent to accreditation of the institution.

The recognition of accrediting associations as legitimate is based on both governmental approval and reciprocity among associations and their member institutions. Accrediting associations are considered legitimate if the member institutions in other associations accept their standards and the credits and diplomas of their member institutions. Reputations of associations are established over time and are a powerful incentive to maintain and improve standards.

The Role of Government

The federal government of the United States is empowered to recognize accrediting associations for the purpose of approving institutions that are permitted to participate in federal student financial assistance programmes. However, the government does not itself accredit any institutions; it only recognizes certain accrediting activities conducted by private accrediting associations. Legitimacy as a nationally recognized accrediting association for post-secondary education is accomplished by meeting the standards for membership in the Council for Higher Education Accreditation and/or the Association of Specialized and Professional Accreditors. The quality assurance standards required of member associations of the Council for Higher Education Accreditation and the Association of Specialized and Professional Accreditors are similar to those required of associations eligible for federal recognition.

Protecting Excellence

Quality assurance involves more than the enforcement of agreed standards of operation. The standards that recognized accrediting associations develop and use to inspect and evaluate institutions and programmes are important, but these are minimum criteria. Meeting those standards means that a school or higher education institution has earned approval from its peers in the US education community. Most educators, however, strive for more than basic recognition. They aim to achieve excellence, a far less definable goal but an important one. The United States belongs to the International Network of Quality Assurance Agencies in Higher Education, a Netherlands-based organization promoting quality assurance programmes and initiatives around the world. Several US accrediting associations are active members of the International Network of Quality Assurance Agencies in Higher Education, as is the Council for Higher Education Accreditation.

Australia

The quality assurance framework for the Australian higher education sector takes into account the country's federal structure, its universities and its history. The country specifically avoided adopting a British model (with what as felt to be its intrusiveness), a US model (which involves industry regulation within a very diverse system) or a European model (with close links between universities and the state). It has established the Australian University Quality Agency as the cornerstone of the framework. Its main role is to verify the claims made by institutions. Its audits and reports constitute the evidence used to assure students, the community and the outside world that Australian universities are of a good standard.

Credibility: The Key

The key to the Australian model is credibility, and such credibility is guaranteed by ensuring that the agency is not beholden to any particular interest group and cannot be compromised in its role. The agency is at a distance from the government: the agency experts are allowed to undertake their audits without fear or favour and the agency produces public reports. This is guaranteed by the agency's constitution. Self-assessment data covering all of the activities undertaken by an institution is major part of the process. The audits by the Australian University Quality Agency focus on how effectively and professionally institutions monitor their own performance and use the information gained for institutional planning and improvement. Audits are based on broad criteria and conducted against each institution's mission, thus encouraging diversity.

Review Focus

Review teams are appointed by the agency to focus on:

- the appropriateness of quality assurance and improvement plans in relation to institutional contexts and missions;
- the rigour of the mechanisms employed to review courses and academic organizational units and to monitor performance against institutional plans;
- research activities and outputs;

  the effectiveness in implementing outcomes of quality assurance processes; and

- the level of communication with stakeholders.

Thus, the Australian system:

- reflects clearly the responsibility of governments to provide a robust quality assurance and accreditation framework;
- recognizes the autonomy of higher education institutions;
- places the responsibility for the quality of provision on individual universities; and
- signals to the community the quality of the higher education system in Australia is assured through a rigorous external audit of university quality assurance processes.

Appendix 2

Information, Documentation and Data Supplied to a Review Team

The information, documentation and data supplied to a review team, before or during the visit, usually includes (but may not be limited to):

- Admissions information and promotional material, concerning the Faculty, department and/or discipline, supplied to prospective students
- Criteria for entry for both programmes and courses
- Full information on each programme and course, in faculty or departmental handbooks, course outlines or otherwise
- Departmental annual reports for the last three years
- Minutes of all staff meetings over the last two years
- Minutes of staff/student liaison committee meetings over the last two years
- Minutes of curriculum review committee meetings over the past two years
- Minutes of Faculty Board meetings over the past two years
- Reports from university and external examiners, where utilized, over the preceding three years, with departmental responses or samples of examination papers, with scripts and mark schemes
- Responses of the department and faculty to these reports
- Examination results for all courses for the preceding three academic years, and for those courses franchised to another institution
- A student profile by gender, at undergraduate and postgraduate levels, including numbers in programmes/courses and students' entry qualifications, for the preceding three academic years
- Numbers graduating from each programme for the preceding three academic years

- Other relevant student statistics (throughput rates, grade distributions, retention rates, class of degrees awarded and so on)
- Evidence of the use of quantitative data in monitoring the teaching/learning process
- Student end-of-course assessment data
- Evidence of student participation in committees/boards of department/faculty
- Outline of procedures for providing students with feedback
- Destination data for graduates of the programmes
- Reports of surveys of graduates
- Reports of surveys of employers
- List of academic staff with individual profiles, including qualifications, level of post, length of service, research interests, recent publications and other relevant information
- Evidence of staff development policies, including identification of staff needs and participation of staff in related activities, including part-time and support staff
- Reports of annual academic staff appraisals by head of department
- Departmental quality assurance handbook
- Evidence of involvement in UWI or other quality assurance procedures

References and Further Reading

American Council on Education. 1997. *Universities and Colleges*, 15th ed. Washington, DC: American Council on Education.

Astin, A. 1991. *Assessment for Excellence: The Philosophy and Practice of Assessment and Evaluation in Higher Education*. New York: American Council on Education/Macmillan Publishing.

Ball, C. 1985. "What the Hell Is Quality?" In *Fitness for Purpose: Essays in Higher Education*. Guildford: Nelson.

Brown, S., and A. Glasner, eds. 1999. *Assessment Matters in Higher Education: Choosing and Using Diverse Approaches*. Buckingham: Society for Research into Higher Education/Open University Press.

Clarke, P.M. 2000. "Quality Assurance and Teacher Professionalism in Higher Education". Paper presented at the conference Uses of Quality Assurance. Centre for Higher Education Research and Information, London.

Deming, W.E. 1982. *Out of the Crisis: Quality, Productivity and Competitive Position*. Cambridge: Cambridge University Press.

Development of Higher Education and Science. 1987. *Higher Education: Meeting the Challenge*. White Paper, Cm 114. London: Her Majesty's Stationery Office.

Development of Higher Education and Science. 1991. *Higher Education: A New Framework*. White Paper, Cm 1541. London: Her Majesty's Stationery Office.

De Wit, P. 1992. *Quality Assurance in University Continuing Vocational Education*. London: Her Majesty's Stationery Office.

Ellis, R., ed. 1993. *Quality Assurance for University Teaching*. Buckingham: Society for Research into Higher Education/Open University Press.

European Commission. 1991. *Memorandum on Higher Education in the European Community* [5 November]. Brussels: Commission of the European Communities.

European Training Foundation. 1998. *Quality Assurance in Higher Education: Final Report and Project Recommendations*. London: European Training Foundation.

Harvey, L., and D. Green. 1993. "Defining Quality". *Assessment and Evaluation in Higher Education* 18, no. 1: 9–34.

London, E. 1994. "Quality Assurance Systems in CARICOM: The Jamaican Perspective". In *The Imperative of Quality Assurance in Tertiary Education*, edited by R.S. Alleyne, 21–31. Port of Spain: NIHERST.

Lucas, C. 1996. *Crisis in the Academy: Rethinking Higher Education in America*. New York: St Martin's Press.

Mazelan P., C. Brannigan, and D. Green. 1991. "Using Measures of Student Satisfaction: The Implications of a User-Led Strategy of Quality Assurance in Higher Education". *Broadcast* [Journal of the Scottish Further Education Unit] 18 (Winter): 4–5.

Palomba, C., and T. Banta. 1999. *Assessment Essentials: Planning, Implementing and Improving Assessment in Higher Education*. San Francisco: Jossey-Bass.

Pirsig, R.M. 1976. *Zen and the Art of Motorcycle Maintenance: An Inquiry into Values*. London: Corgi.

Politt, C. 1990. "Doing Business in the Temple? Managers and Quality Assurance in the Public Services". *Public Administration* 68 (Winter): 435–52.

Roberts, D., and T. Higgins. 1992. *Higher Education: The Student Experience. The Findings of a Research Programme into Student Decision Making and Consumer Satisfaction*. Leeds: HEIST.

Robbins, L. 1963. *Report of the Committee on Higher Education*. Cm 2154. London: Her Majesty's Stationery Office.

Sallis, E. 1996. *Total Quality Management in Education*, 2d ed. London: Kogan Page.

Scott, P., ed. 1998. *The Globalization of Higher Education*. Buckingham: Society for Research into Higher Education/Open University Press.

Stone, J. 1997. *Increasing Effectiveness: A Guide to Quality Management*. London: Falmer Press.

Taylor, W. 1981. "Quality Control? Analysis and Comment". *Educational Administration* 9, no. 2: 1–20.

United States Department of Education. National Center for Education Statistics. 1996/97. Washington, DC.

University of the West Indies. 2000. *Official Statistics*. Mona, Jamaica: University of the West Indies.

University of the West Indies. Chancellor's Commission on the Governance of UWI. 1994. *A New Structure: The Regional University in the 1990s and Beyond*. Mona, Jamaica: University of the West Indies.

University of the West Indies. Office of the Board for Undergraduate Studies. 1997. *Status Report on Issues Regarding Articulation with TLIs*. Mona, Jamaica: University of the West Indies.

University of the West Indies. Office of the Board for Undergraduate Studies. 2000a. *The UWI Quality Strategy*. Mona, Jamaica: University of the West Indies.

University of the West Indies. Office of the Board for Undergraduate Studies. 2000b. *Quality Assurance at the University of the West Indies: The Self-Assessment*, 4th ed. Mona, Jamaica: University of the West Indies.

University of the West Indies. Tertiary Level Institutions Unit. 1997. *UWI/TLI Relationships: Rationalising and Formalising Arrangements*. Cave Hill, Barbados: University of the West Indies.

University of the West Indies. Tertiary Level Institutions Unit. 1998. *Collaboration between UWI and Other Regional Tertiary Level Institutions*. Cave Hill, Barbados: University of the West Indies.

Vroeijenstjin, T.I. 1991. "External Quality Assessment: Servant of Two Masters?" Paper presented to the Conference on Quality Assurance in Higher Education. Hong Kong, 15–17 July.

Walsh, K. 1991. "Quality and Public Services". *Public Administration* 69, no. 4: 503–14.

Weert, E. de. 1990. "A Macro Analysis of Quality Assessment in Higher Education". *Higher Education* 19: 57–72.

Whiteley, P. 1997. "Quality Assurance at the University of the West Indies." *Caribbean Journal of Education* 19, no. 2: 191–210.

Whiteley, P. 1999. *Quality Assurance and Quality Audit at the University of the West Indies: Procedures and Practices*. Mona, Jamaica: Office of the Board for Undergraduate Studies, University of the West Indies.

Whiteley, P. 2000a. "Assessing the Quality of Distance Education: The Case of the University of the West Indies". In *Proceedings of the Conference on Distance Education in Small States*, 240–47. Cave Hill, Barbados: Distance Education Centre, University of the West Indies.

Whiteley, P. 2000b. "The University of the West Indies and Caribbean Tertiary Level Institutions: Increasing Access, Maintaining Quality". *Journal of Education and Development in the Caribbean* 4, no. 1: 41–52.

World Bank. 2000. *Task Force on Higher Education: Peril and Promise*. Washington, DC: World Bank.

www.ingramcontent.com/pod-product-compliance
Lightning Source LLC
Chambersburg PA
CBHW062131160426
43191CB00013B/2263